BECOMING ADAPTABLE

Pre-publication praise for *Becoming Adaptable*

The journey of becoming is both challenging and to be enjoyed. Although we cannot predict our final destination, we can guide ourselves through making strategic decisions and learning from everything we do along our unique path. OrgZoo creative metaphor is a delightful way to titillate our thought and expand our consciousness. Another winning book by Dr Arthur Shelley!

> *Dr Alex Bennet, Director, Mountain Quest Institute; Professor, IKI Southeast Asia, Bangkok University; former Chief Knowledge Officer, Department of the Navy, USA*

William Arthur Ward was somewhat famous for his quote "The pessimist complains about the wind; the optimist expects it to change; the realist adjusts the sails." But what exactly does that look like in face of the pressures we face every day? Surely it is more than just being resilient. Complexity theory showed us that the nature of being adaptable is far more than just doing certain things or taking various actions.

There is a complex interplay, a dance we need to enter with the forces around us. Dr Shelley's new book takes this one step further and deeper. When we switch our focus to the actual journey of *Becoming Adaptable* — not just within oneself, but also as part of the teams and communities we are members of. We don't just gain flexibility; we also unlock the amazing power of cocreation. Arthur calls us not just to readjust our sails, he shows how those currents that might dash us on the rocks can also propel us to our destination faster than the strongest rowers ever could.

> *Stuart French, Program Manager, Knowledge. Victorian Country Fire Authority, Australia*

Praise for Becoming Adaptable

The pandemic made us realise that there is no such thing as a stable comfort zone. We are on a journey, like the one described by famous Greek poet Cavafy in his 1975 poem *Ithaka*. Giving a purpose to our lives, finding our own Ithaka, by facilitating interactions with a positive impact, can help us become adaptable and create a better life. Humans can create miracles if they choose to do so. *Becoming Adaptable* and innovative is an excellent start. The learning facilitation activities in this book will enable readers to adapt their capabilities, to become more confident, innovative, better connected, and of course more adaptable.

Dr Margarita Kefalaki, President, Communication Institute of Greece (COMinG)

The times of chaos, crisis and rapid change require us to adapt to our environment. Behavioural adaptability helps us not only to be conscious, but to proactively manage our behavioural interactions in the world of diverse culture, for better results.

Kholane Clarkeson Chauke, Senior Specialist Knowledge Management, Industry Development Corporation of South Africa; Knowledge Management South Africa (KMSA)

Being adaptable is essential in our new world, whether changes are enforced on us or when we are involved in initiating them. This book provides ideas and methods to be more adaptable; however, by doing so, it suggests more, including ideas on how to develop personal skills (eg decision making) and social skills (eg conflict resolution). Arthur Shelley does excellent work in leading us on this journey.

Dr Moria Levy, CEO ROM Knowledgeware, Israel; ISO 30401 standard leader; Author of A Holistic Approach to Lessons Learned

BECOMING ADAPTABLE

The development of artists requires curiosity, courage and adaptability; getting out of comfort zone enhances creativity and is critical to success.

> *Brigitte Carbonneau, Head of Artistic Services, Cirque du Soleil Entertainment Group, Canada*

The need for technical expertise is often acknowledged by organisational leaders given transformation and digitalisation disruptions. The need for adaptive expertise, however, has only recently entered our consciousness, emphasised by the pandemic and its impact on the way we will need to think, act and feel differently. *Becoming Adaptable* is a timely and valuable guide to steering us through the many choices and commitments ahead of us, as we work to become more successful leaders in this challenging new normal.

> *Dr Karuna Ramanathan, Transformation Consultant-Coach, KR Konsulting Singapore.*
> *Author of* Navigating the Seas of Change

Experience has shown me that adaptability and behavioural awareness are critical success factors in life, especially in a diverse mixture of cultures. Behavioural adaptability helps us not just to be aware, but to proactively manage our interactions and relationships with others, for better outcomes in everything we do, personally and in business.

> *Dr Juan Román, Space Science and Engineering Director at SAIC. Former Deputy Director of Engineering at NASA's Goddard Space Flight Center, USA*

Praise for Becoming Adaptable

Our choices set the path our lives will take. Not choosing is not an option. After the coronavirus pandemic, old ways of being will never return, the new ways are unknown. Are we ready for never being ready? Are we prepared to make choices in a totally unpredictable world? *Becoming Adaptable* can help us to better understand ourselves in this coming 'new' world, so that we can make more assertive choices and have a lighter and more fruitful journey.

Dr Rose Longo, Professor of Design Thinking and Creative Leadership, FIAP, Brazil

The title Becoming Adaptable resonates with me as a realistic optimist: optimism is the underpinning trait of the adaptable person powering innovation and resilience. Arthur is spot on as he includes optimism as a "fundamental to getting positive outcomes from facilitated activities." So too, in my experience, my behaviour in asking "what makes you optimistic?" is the first time someone is asked to reflect on their optimism. Arthur tells us, "The world will become a better place when everyone learns how to choose their behaviour" — how right he is!

Victor Perton, Founder, The Center for Optimism, Australia. Author of Optimism, The How and Why

Building *ba* (shared time and space) has been the central focus of a Japanese knowledge management approach. Conversations are at the heart of how people build effective *ba* that helps teams and organisations share and cocreate knowledge. *Becoming Adaptable* is rightly built around facilitating inclusive conversations that elevate us to new possibilities in such an uncertain era.

Naoki Ogiwara, Managing Director, Knowledge Associates Japan; IMSAP Director, Japan Innovation Network

BECOMING ADAPTABLE

Perfect timing for the latest book of Dr Arthur Shelley on adaptability. The 2020 COVID-19 pandemic situation made all of us realise the need and value of being adaptable at all levels of society, from the individual to the international levels. Adaptability is no longer an option — it becomes a must in our VUCA world. Inadaptability leads us to remain prisoner of the past. In contrast, adaptability is a foundation of creativity and a necessary ingredient in innovation (creating the future). So, if you are interested in better understanding and mastering the concepts, behaviours and practices leading to adaptability, this great book will help you to achieve that and may become a life changer for you.

Dr Vincent Ribiere, Managing Director and Co-Founder of the Institute for Knowledge and Innovation Southeast Asia (IKI-SEA), Bangkok University, Thailand

Constant changes evolve new norms and trends and expectations. Growing competition and changes in customer behaviour are intense winds shaking our ship through stormy seas. Adaptation enables the application of our knowledge to reset sails and safely navigate to new destinations. Many companies come into the market with great ideas, but few reach unshakeable leader positions because they lack adaptability. Inspiring the team's ability to sense changes, adapt their mindset and actions towards new realities while remaining goal-oriented, is one of the best investments a leader can make. This book will guide leaders and individuals on their way to salute change as a positive catalyst and gain positioning from it.

Vadim Shiryaev, Managing Partner, Trout & Partners, Russia

Praise for Becoming Adaptable

A boost in creativity is directly linked to people happiness. Simply feeling like a part of a collaborative team makes us more motivated. This is really clear in school or university when students and teachers are involved together in pedagogical innovation where cocreation is stimulated by codesign such as in flipped classrooms. Adaptability accelerates all these activities.

Dr Jean-Charles Cailliez, HDR, Directeur HEMiSF4iRE Design School, Vice-Président Innovation de l'Université Catholique de Lille, France

Insightful. Incisive. Intuitive: *Becoming Adaptable* is perfect for purpose-driven people looking to develop intentional, focused and embedded behaviours to enhance leadership through uncertain times. It offers a truly engaging, understandable framework to discover and apply a practical approach to achieve measurable outcomes today and well into the future.

Alexander Boome, Program Director, Hinrich Foundation, Singapore

Most of our beliefs are fixed but not founded on any rational evidence. Thus, *Becoming Adaptable* means questioning everything we believe and being prepared to change our views and behaviours. It means engaging with others in conversation with an open mind, regardless of what you think of them or their ideas. This willingness to change is at the heart of OrgZoo thinking. I highly recommend this book.

David Gurteen, Founder Gurteen Knowledge Community; Author, Conversational Leadership. UK

BECOMING ADAPTABLE

While agility and adaptability have been discussed in organisational circles for quite some time now, the whole approach has been accelerated during the pandemic — which seems to be rippling across the world through successive waves. At an individual and organisational level, we all need to be more resilient and adaptable — not just more productive and innovative. Drawing on his earlier works in organisational behaviour and knowledge management, Arthur Shelley shares valuable insights on the frameworks, impacts, nuts and bolts of adaptability. From conversational skills to behavioural change, the book offers practical tips and tools for organisational leaders.

> Dr Madanmohan Rao, Research Director, YourStory Media, India.; Co-author, Communities of Innovation: How Organisations Harness Collective Creativity and Build Resilience

I have used Organizational Zoo techniques since their introduction over ten years ago. Initially they appealed to me as a safe and accessible way for people to understand their own behaviour and that of others. It has proved to be just that and more... helping people to grapple with behaviour in the face of increasing uncertainty and complexity and helping them to shift and shape their behaviour to achieve better outcomes for everyone.

> Laurel Sutton, Principal, Creative Cognicion, and Collaborative Partner, Complexability Australia

An entrepreneurial start-up would never get started, nor become a success, if it were not highly adaptable. The more adaptable we become, the more success we can achieve. Many of the most successful businesses in the world have achieved their leadership status through their adaptability and willingness to act differently.

> Harry Ma, Senior lawyer of Beijing Dentons Law Offices LLP, Chair at the Australia China Entrepreneurs Dialogue

I find that the OrgZoo concept brings about powerful generative conversations. Having utilised it when facilitating retreats and in volunteer work, I find that it has the power to positively impact how people interact, behave and make informed choices. Arthur himself 'walks' his work in always expanding the dialogue to accept divergent views for wider choices. I commend his expanding body of work to support personal and overall transformation.

NC Prakash Vice President, Human Resources (Asia Pacific), Rohde & Schwarz

Lifelong learning is essential for us to remain relevant, and this requires adaptability. In the constantly changing and dynamic world of international trade, being adaptable helps people build trust which is at the heart of sustainable relationships. Thoughtful, perceptive, astute, Becoming Adaptable and its importance in success, especially in the modern world of volatility, uncertainty, complexity, and ambiguity (VUCA), facilitates us to elevate our awareness and actions towards these results. Future global trade leaders must constantly adapt and would benefit greatly from the concepts offered in this book. I wish I would have been able to read this book a few years ago, when mistakes I made would likely have gone differently with the insight and understanding of Organizational Zoo, applied social learning ecosystems, Conversations That Matter and *KNOWledge SUCCESSion*! I will be incorporating these concepts to both global trade academic, and professional networks.

Dr Steve Clarke, Co-Founder of the Master of Global Trade, HCMC, Vietnam

BECOMING ADAPTABLE

Becoming Adaptable

by Dr Arthur Shelley

Illustrated by Dr Mark Boyes

Published by Intelligent Answers Pty Ltd

Melbourne, Australia

Intelligent Answers Pty Ltd
www.intelligentanswers.com.au

ISBN 978-0-6484616-3-0 (print)
ISBN 978-0-6484616-4-7 (ebook)

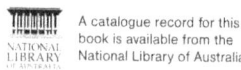
A catalogue record for this book is available from the National Library of Australia

Copyright © 2021 Arthur W Shelley

All rights reserved. No part of this publication may be reproduced, stored in a retrieval system or transmitted in any form or by any means, electronic, mechanical, photocopy, recording or otherwise, without prior written permission from Intelligent Answers, Melbourne, Australia with the exception of short excerpts used with acknowledgment of publisher and author.

Cover design by Dr Mark Boyes
Illustrations by Dr Mark Boyes and Dr Arthur Shelley
Editing by Margaret L Ruwoldt
Book design (print and epub) by Margaret L Ruwoldt

Published in Melbourne, Australia

Dedication

Everyone knows that adaptability is important for success and wellbeing.

However, very few know how to become adaptable.

Becoming Adaptable involves being open to others' ideas and actively exploring a diversity of concepts.

This book provides practical approaches to develop your own adaptability and to assist others improve theirs.

BECOMING ADAPTABLE

Preface

We are all on a journey of becoming.

Each experience changes you slightly, either confirming or challenging your current patterns and beliefs. When you reflect on what you want to become, you are more likely to adjust your compass and make choices that lead to better outcomes.

I believe in self-determination: taking responsibility for what you achieve through your journey. Many people have fewer opportunities and less freedom of choice, and this injustice is something to rectify in our shared world. However, at some level, we are each capable of making choices.

Each of us has a comfort zone where we cling to familiar patterns and perceptions. Using self-challenges and reflective contemplation, you can develop the ability to make choices outside your comfort zone and achieve better outcomes in the longer term. *Becoming Adaptable* is about consistently building your repertoire of knowledge, skills and (mostly) behavioural capabilities to optimise

BECOMING ADAPTABLE

your choices. It challenges you to reflect (ideally before you make a decision) on why you behave in the ways you do.

We all have subconscious biases that guide our behaviour unless we consciously choose otherwise. As you build confidence and grow your comfort zone, you open more options for future possibilities. Engaging in conversation with trusted mentors will help you to make better choices and develop a greater repertoire of behavioural capabilities.

Trusted conversations and reflective practice will build your conscious understanding of yourself and others, making you more capable as an individual and professional.

The 2020 coronavirus pandemic demonstrated the importance of being adaptable to achieve optimal outcomes. Initially people felt a strong pull to 'return to normal' and became stressed that leaders and officials were unable to provide a clear answer. The truth is, after such a monumental crisis, the world does not return to the old ways of doing things. Individuals, teams, relationships and the world generally have been transformed: going back to the limitations of former comfort zones is no longer satisfying — or, in some cases, possible.

Whilst some will yearn for the normal past, I believe reflective people will seek a 'new normal.' The challenges we faced, and continue to confront, have brought us to a higher level of capability and a desire to do some things differently in the future. Humanity evolves over time and a crisis accelerates this evolution.

The best way to prepare for inevitable change is to proactively evolve yourself, stretching your comfort zone before being forced to. That way, when a change inevitably comes, you will cope with it better than those who seek stability and comfort from a (fictional) status quo. Prior to the COVID-19 pandemic most office workers were reluctant to interact virtually. Now we are more comfortable with interacting online, companies are more open to employees

Preface

working flexible hours from home, we are a little more comfortable in isolation, and our dogs expect those extra daily walks. Although we did not arrive at this juncture willingly, we could have. Now that we have been forced to be more adaptable, we can see the benefits of being better prepared for the next change.

When we understand how to make choices about behaviour, we start to approach change in a more proactive way. Instead of reacting to unpredictability with panic, we can take appropriate actions to regain a sense of control. We manage what can be managed and we monitor and prepare contingencies for the things outside our control.

How we behave is a fundamental characteristic of being human, but it is not a fixed feature of each individual. The scope of our behaviours can be modified, learnt and improved upon if learning facilitators offer a safe physical, psychological and social environment for people to explore and learn from each other.

The world has mostly operated on competition in the past, but this just divides humanity. *Becoming Adaptable* enables us to evolve our relationships with more collaboration. Imagine what we could achieve together if we strive for mutual benefits that are fairly distributed.

I believe that the world will become a better place when everyone learns how to choose their behaviour in ways that respect differences, align behaviours, build trusted relationships around common concerns, and leverage differences to fuel creativity and drive innovation. (The OrgZoo website has articles on these topics: see the list of references.)

Becoming Adaptable is a way of learning to consciously, competently, and confidently navigate your life's journey. I hope you will join with me and the members of the Organizational Zoo Ambassador Network (OZAN) as we encourage others to engage in *Becoming Adaptable*.

Dr Arthur W Shelley
September 2021

BECOMING ADAPTABLE

Contents

Preface **15**

Introduction... **23**

    Our cocreated future 25
    Grow yourself and develop others...................................... 26

Part A Understanding the power of adaptability

1. Why is behavioural adaptability important? **29**

    People don't have enough constructive conversations
    about behaviour.. 29
    Behaviour considered as an asset 31
    Seeing difference as opportunity, not conflict.................... 31
    Making the world a better place 35

2. Who becomes adaptable? **39**

    Everyone behaves, or misbehaves, depending
    on perspective 39
    We are human because we consciously socialise 40
    Everyone is a stakeholder of your behaviour 43

3. What is achieved by being adaptable? **49**

    Interactive social learning to cocreate value and build
    relationships 54
    Why games work 55
    Fun-damentals 56

4. When should we facilitate adaptability development? . **61**

    When is an OrgZoo interaction most effective? 64

**5. Where does behavioural adaptability apply
to success?**.. **71**

    Where are behavioural patterns in big business? 75

Part B: How to start becoming adaptable

6. How to facilitate interactions with positive impact **85**

    The OrgZoo approach to engaging interactions................ 85
    Great ideas are stimulated and nurtured from insights 87

BECOMING ADAPTABLE

    The structure of Conversations That Matter 87
    Designing and facilitating effective interactions 90
    Design insights 91
    Facilitation insights 94
    Guiding principles for OrgZoo facilitation 100
    Elevating participation 102

7. Examples of facilitation activities 105

    Activity 7.1 OrgZoo Character Introductions 109
    Activity 7.2 Behavioural DNA 114
    Activity 7.3 Behavioural Improvisation 126
    Activity 7.4 Behavioural Role-Plays 130
    Activity 7.5 Behaviour Matching in Context 137
    Activity 7.6 Stakeholder Assessment 144
    Activity 7.7 Exploring connected foundations of
    culture clash, innovation and cultural transformation 150

8. Tools for efficiency and effectiveness 159

    OrgZoo character cards 161
    Online profiler 163
    Conversations That Matter 167
    Your mind, your mindset, and your behaviour 168
    Video guides 169
    Frequently asked questions (FAQ) 170
    Smartphone app? 170

Part C: Theories and philosophies behind this approach

9. The Organizational Zoo 177

    A brief history of OrgZoo time 177
    Using creative metaphor for understanding behaviour 178
    OrgZoo today 179
    OrgZoo Ambassador Network 180
    OrgZoo Practitioners 181
    OrgZoo Ambassadors 182
    Stories of impact from OrgZoo interactions 182

10 Theories embedded into OrgZoo philosophies 187

    It's fun, practical and yet academically sound 187
    Scientific proof? 189
    Primary influences 196
    Secondary influences 204

Contents

The power of visualisation for creative cocreation 205
Ethical facilitation 207

11. MindFLEX — the complexity of parallel perspective facilitation 213

Part D: Start becoming adaptable for YOU

12. Behaviour can be an asset or a liability 223

Behaviour influences social connections in both directions 223
Consciously choosing and reflecting on your behaviour for greater impact 229
Understanding others' behaviour for greater influence 231

13. Your journey of becoming 239

Knowing how to proactively engage in becoming 239
Doing activities that generate success 240
Becoming a leader and mentor to create your legacy 242

14. Lifestyle learning and value generation for others ... 249

Lifestyle learning to achieve your optimal social contributions 250
Developing beyond yourself to lead others 250
Organizational Zoo Ambassadors Network (OZAN) 251
Leading and inspiring willing intelligent followers 252
Facilitating a safe-fail environment to build sustained trust 252
Being part of developing new learning experiences and approaches 253
Becoming adaptable 254

Appendix: Concepts useful to professional facilitators . 259

Acknowledgements 285

References 280

About the author 295

About the illustrator 297

BECOMING ADAPTABLE

Success stories:

Building awareness of the power of diversity 37

Observing group dynamics through the lens
of OrgZoo 45

Harmonising collaboration and competition to
increase sales 58

Working with change — a Hong Kong example 68

Indonesian Banking organisation 78

Facilitating behavioural conversations in
IT development 171

Building behavioural adaptability in construction 184

Thai business scale-up 209

Applying OrgZoo to shift mindsets 217

The University Zoo 235

Life changing behaviour 244

The Singapore 50-year celebration project 256

Introduction

Human success so often requires us to collaborate on achieving outcomes that no one person alone could have achieved, from simple things like sharing the workload of a small task in a work environment, through to sending people into space and safely returning them to Earth.

We are so much more powerful when we collaborate and so destructive when we engage in conflict. Choosing how to behave makes a significant difference to what value we create or destroy in the world. Behaviour is how we outwardly express our feelings and desires, how we show our respect (or display disrespect) and is the basis of the relationships we form and maintain (or destroy).

This book is about how to become more consciously aware of your own behaviour and how to make deliberate choices about how to behave in different situations. Importantly, this book is also about how to help others adopt an adaptable mindset.

Becoming Adaptable was conceived as a manual of activities for use by facilitators who seek highly interactive approaches to engage

BECOMING ADAPTABLE

participants in deep social learning. This idea evolved into a reference guide for a range of activities that can be used to develop behavioural competencies. There are too many variants of the techniques to describe them all in one book. However, the most commonly used activities are described in detail here so that competent facilitators can apply them across a range of contexts.

This is also a book for learning designers, coaches and consultants who work with groups, teams and executives. Identifying desired behaviours and adapting to emerging conditions is an essential enterprise skill in an increasingly complex world.

The Organizational Zoo creative metaphor is central to *Becoming Adaptable*. The OrgZoo fosters a growing level of comfort across the spectrum of behavioural options and contexts. It helps us to consciously choose our behaviours and align them to present and future contexts. This enables us to lead people (organizationalzoo.com/behavioural-dna-of-leadership) towards better decisions and to create applied social learning ecosystems (journals.sfu.ca/jalt/index.php/jalt/article/ view/19) that are richer and more sustainable.

Along with the Org Zoo concept, several techniques described in this book are taken from my earlier writing, for example:

— Conversations That Matter (organizationalzoo.com/conversations-that-matter)

— creative friction (linkedin.com/pulse/creative-friction-arthur-shelley)

— and the learning mindset from my book *KNOWledge SUCCESSion* (2017)

Throughout this book you will find foundational themes relevant to successfully facilitating activities around *Becoming Adaptable*. These are covered in some detail in Part B and assume that people will be open to a shift in mindset from 'extraction' (taking from society) towards 'how do I contribute to society and share value in a fair way?'

Introduction

Although adaptability can be used for self-interest, the ideas in this book are shared to encourage people to create a more sustainable society and a resilient global ecosystem that supports everyone.

Our cocreated future

Behaviour is an essential human characteristic. We behave in everything we do. Some behaviour is learned from the day you were born and some is genetic. Whatever its origin, behaviour is usually an unconscious thing — it seems to just happen.

The *Becoming Adaptable* approach enables groups of people to collectively explore which behaviours will lead to optimal outcomes in a particular context. To do this, we use the Organizational Zoo metaphor.

The OrgZoo is a collection of 27 common behaviours, each represented by an animal. OrgZoo activities use these fictional characters to explore human behaviour objectively, cocreating a common understanding of what is possible and appropriate. Of course, with humans there are differences of opinion. OrgZoo distinguishes between the person and their behaviour, allowing a neutral dialogue that builds relationships rather than damages them.

When people engage in safe conversations about behaviour, they are in a learning mode like no other. They socialise different perceptions in ways that are unachievable in other approaches. All of the OrgZoo activities are deliberately cocreative: there are no predetermined answers. In each activity the participants collaborate to create outputs and generate outcomes. This approach not only shares the collective knowledge and perceptions of the participants: it generates new knowledge and insights. Collaborative conversations facilitated before, during, and after the OrgZoo activities will extend the value created. This nurtures relationships, trust and other intangible benefits that flow from the interactions.

BECOMING ADAPTABLE

Grow yourself and develop others

This book can help you become better at what you wish to be. Being adaptable means meeting challenges with enthusiasm and an open mind. It allows you adjust your approach and select from a broader range of options to make the most of any situation. Confidence and resilience stem from knowing you have selected the optimal path. Circumstances may change unexpectedly, but an adaptable person has contingent options at hand to deal with whatever happens. Whilst this does not guarantee success in every endeavour, your adaptability optimises your learning when things don't go to plan. You'll perform better the next time around.

You can get involved in *Becoming Adaptable* in many ways. The most obvious is reading, reflecting and applying the concepts in the book for your own development. The more you practise, the more adaptable you become. Getting started as an OrgZoo practitioner, whether it be for self-development, social development or to be used as a commercial tool, is simple enough. To extend yourself, join the OrgZoo Ambassadors Network (OZAN) practitioners forum or enrol in the practitioners masterclass for a deeper and wider understanding of the techniques and how to facilitate them.

Perhaps you are already quite adaptable and want to help others to become adaptable. OrgZoo adds engaging, playful concepts to your existing set of tools and techniques as a leader, mentor or coach. Just be sure to read the sections on ethical facilitation and understand the underlying design principles so that you can act in the best possible way and for the right reasons.

Understanding behaviour and how it influences your life is a critical part of being adaptable. The better you become at recognising behaviours and confidently choosing from a wider range of behavioural options, the more likely you are to be successful. My experiences, and those of the OZAN members, show that OrgZoo is a great way to accelerate your progress in *Becoming Adaptable*.

Part A
Understanding the power of adaptability

BECOMING ADAPTABLE

1. Why is behavioural adaptability important?

People don't have enough constructive conversations about behaviour

Aren't we adaptable enough already?

Truth is, we are not. The world seems to be speeding up. With technological advances and changes in societal expectations, by the time something becomes a new pattern that we can predict and feel comfortable with, everything has changed. Even the World Economic Forum changes its list of the key future skills every five years. Over the past three WEF Future of Jobs reports (weforum.org/reports/the-future-of-jobs-report-2020), some foundational capabilities like critical thinking have remained at the top of the list. Others have disappeared. The list is shifting more towards 'soft skills' and intangibles, leaving behind traditional 'hard' or 'scientific' management skills. World leaders increasingly see behaviour, and

BECOMING ADAPTABLE

the ability to deeply understand your own and that of others, as critical to future prosperity.

As you will come to discover in this book, the best way to learn how to become adaptable and develop your behavioural capabilities is through conversations. If you want to win a decathlon you train hard, getting fitter and developing your strengths across a wide range of capabilities. The modern social world is similar. Things change so often and so fast, we can never be quite sure of what challenges we will face and who will stand with or against us. Success in this environment requires constant adaptation, just to be prepared for the next unpredictable shift.

Constructive conversations about perceptions and behaviours are difficult for many people. Imagine the scenario: your boss says to you, "OK, let's go back to my office and discuss your behaviour." Clearly an invitation that no one wants to receive. That conversation is already one you want to decline (if you can get away with that). There's an immediate feeling of caution, even dread.

What if that invitation was instead helpful and perhaps even fun to engage in?

Imagine yourself engaging in satisfying conversations about the interactions between people; conversations where everyone is constructively participating and being open. Just how good can we become if we share perspectives in a way that everyone learns from?

So, no. We do not have enough Conversations That Matter (as described in my book *KNOWledge SUCCESSion*) around the topic of behaviour. Becoming an elite athlete takes a lot of invested passion and energy but, with moderate effort, everyone can move to a better level of general fitness. Not everyone can become a champion of constructive conversations and behavioural maturity, but we can all benefit from more of them in our lives.

1. Why is behavioural adapability important?

Behaviour considered as an asset

What happens when you really need to know something? If you work as a loner, you will probably conduct an internet search and get *the* answer from the first page of results. Even though search results are skewed by advertising and promoted content, this approach is quick and acceptable to most people in a hurry.

A far better option is to ask a group of trusted friends what they think. Instead of getting *the* (promoted) answer, you listen to a constructive discussion about the many possibilities. Socialising among a diverse group of people is a powerful way to get ideas and insights, not only from existing knowledge and experiences but by opening the possibility of cocreating ideas and knowledge (Shelley 2020b).

Effective socialisation of ideas depends on having a trusted community to socialise with. Trusted communities arise over time as you actively collaborate with people who, through their positive experiences in these interactions, wish to engage further with you in the future. Like trust itself, these relationships can be severely damaged very quickly by inappropriate behaviour. Appropriate behaviour aligned to a common set of values is the foundation of a collaborative community. In this sense, behaviour is an asset that is required to enable a flow of knowledge between people that stimulates open conversations, accelerates creativity and ultimately drives innovation.

If you can enable people to become more adaptable in their behavioural choices, you create a lever to accelerate knowledge flow and culture change. These are essential ingredients for success in our volatile, uncertain, complex and ambiguous (VUCA) world (Deaton 2018).

Seeing difference as opportunity, not conflict

Human history is full of examples of conflict over differences of perspectives. Leaders have engaged in conflicts to protect themselves from others, or to invade and control others.

BECOMING ADAPTABLE

Typically, people will be more inclined to collaborate with those they consider 'us' or insiders, and compete with those they consider 'them' or outsiders (Crisp 2015). What differentiates us from others? Are these differences clear? Are they based on assumptions or do we have first-hand evidence that these differences are absolute and real?

Although modern society is vast, sophisticated and increasingly global in perspective, in evolutionary terms our behavioural capabilities are much the same as they were thousands of years ago. Competition may be more appropriate in a static ecosystem, where resources are scarcer, while collaboration is more effective in a rapidly changing environment. This is not an either/or equation: a thriving, sustainable society needs a balance of both modes (see Figure 1.1).

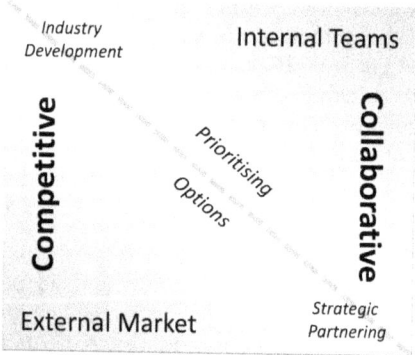

Figure 1.1. Achieving harmony between competition and collaboration

The challenge is to get more people more comfortable with collaboration and the benefits it brings, both personally and professionally. The same principle applies at all scales, from families and social groups to companies and countries. Being adaptable and open-minded enables us to make better choices about when to compete and when to collaborate.

1. Why is behavioural adapability important?

From the day we are born, we are continually reminded that being the best at something attracts attention and kudos. In the western world in particular, individualism is celebrated, and this creates a strong capability set in conflict (the ability to win and be the star).

In contrast, collaborating with others is often dismissed as weakness or, worse, condemned as cheating. The word 'collaborator' conjures images of betrayal and working with the enemy. Manipulating a market through insider trading is an example of collaboration without an ethical basis.

This is unfortunate because collaborative behaviours are far better suited to the modern world. For example, collaboration in a global pandemic created several effective vaccines far more quickly than traditional drug development processes. Collaboration leverages many more perspectives than competition, and exploring the differences of perspective can generate more possibilities for action.

When you have a competing mindset and are confident in your ability to win, your knowledge represents a competitive advantage over others. Highly competitive companies legally register their knowledge as intellectual property, actively preventing others from using it. Knowledge becomes a highly controlled source of income as companies mete it out to selected candidates. This 'winner takes all' mentality can generate a disparity of wealth in society. Where there are winners who continually extract and hoard wealth, there is also an underclass of people who are the source of labour to be exploited by the winners. This 'extraction mindset' is generally unsustainable in the longer term. The capitalist system goes through boom and build cycles, but eventually must crash when resources are depleted.

Modern westernised capitalism teaches us how to compete, but not how to collaborate. Many leaders do not know how to harmonise the alternative ways forward. Exacerbating the challenge is our strong focus on maximising short term value extraction: the tyranny of the election cycle or the demand for projects to deliver 'quick

BECOMING ADAPTABLE

wins'. Imagine what we could achieve together if we were as skilled at collaboration as we are at competition.

Being competitive usually means doing the same thing faster and cheaper. Successful collaboration is based on the power of many. When ideas from multiple people and perspectives are shared and bounced around in conversations, they mutate and generate new possibilities that simply will not occur in competition.

Specialist vegetable farmers can compete with each other, spruiking their own brand of vegetables as the best available. Alternatively, they can collaborate to produce a mixed vegetable soup that appeals to a much broader market. This may sound socialist, but it makes commercial sense as well. Every moment and resource we spend to be competitive does not deliver as much value as combining resources to accelerate growth. If just half of the global military budget were invested in renewable energy research, the world's sustainability issues would be solved in a few years.

People think that competing is the natural state of the human psyche. However, we can learn to place value on a different set of behaviours.

Imagine a world where all the kudos was given to people who contributed to society, rather than extracted from it. A world where Nobel scientists were the names on everyone's lips, rather than someone who can make the greatest profit from online retailing. This world would have heroes and role models who add value to society in everything they do, rather than becoming wealthy at the expense of others.

What about philanthropy? Some wealthy people are extremely generous to selected charities, social enterprises and small start-ups. Does this make up for the way that wealth was accumulated? How much 'giving back' is enough? Do we need everything we extract, or does it become an ego game after you have covered your basic needs

1. Why is behavioural adapability important?

(as meagre or extravagant as these may be). In the words of Ricardo Semler, "If you need to give back, then you took too much."

I am not advocating that we replace competitive skills with collaborative capabilities. Rather, we need a better balance. We can evolve towards treating collaboration and competition as equal partners, like *yin* and *yang*, to create a society that is more harmonious and resilient.

British colonisers considered themselves superior to Australia's Indigenous peoples because they were stronger and had better weapons. They took over management of the country because they believed they could make it more productive and there was value to be extracted. The reality is that Indigenous peoples had lived in harmony with the land and practised sophisticated ecosystem management for at least 60,000 years. It took less than 200 years of the colonisers' extraction mindset to destroy settlements and agricultural practices, upset habitats, and make many species extinct.

How different things might have been if the invading British had arrived with the intention of learning how to live sustainably

in a new environment and alongside existing cultures. It's impossible to know for sure, but it seems likely a more collaborative approach by the colonists would have resulted in a very different modern Australia.

Making the world a better place

What does making the world a better place mean to you? Fairer, more sustainable, happier, more energised, richer? While the answer is different for each of us, we have this in common: *Becoming Adaptable* will increase your chances of achieving your desired outcomes.

In an unbalanced society, those with the inclination and motivation to change the world do not have the power. Those with the power to change the world neither have the inclination nor the motivation.

BECOMING ADAPTABLE

Behavioural adaptability reduces the gap between motivation and power. It gives you resilience to deal with the uncertainty of modern living. Knowing you have choices, and having confidence in your decisions, enables you to interact better in a range of situations. Applying the activities in this book will help you to become adaptable, so that you can influence your world in the direction you would like to see it evolve.

Think about the bigger challenges we face and the behaviours we need to address them. Are we adequately collaborative and adaptable?

Do we manage the Earth for humans? Is that all humans or just some special ones? Who gets the right to decide that? What about animals, plants and our general ecosystem and climate patterns? Are they just there of our benefit, or do they have some rights too?

What are the short-term and longer-term implications of how we behave and the decisions we make? Are we trying to preserve what we have, regenerate the system to what it was, or improve our shared home to become a better place for all?

Questions like these highlight many behavioural shortcomings among humans the world over. Despite everything, I retain a high degree of optimism about humanity and our ability to cocreate a better world. We just need to become adaptable and focus on optimal long-term outcomes.

SUCCESS STORY
Building awareness of the power of diversity

Netpreeya Kate Choomchaiyo
OZAN Ambassador, Thailand

Context (where and when)

Leadership workshops using OrgZoo have been conducted in a large Thailand organisation since 2018. The program was designed to assist participants to recognise their true potential. The OrgZoo was used as a key learning tool in module 'embracing diversity'.

Why

The 'embracing diversity' module was designed to help the participants recognise the differences in personalities, thoughts, perspectives, values and experiences of self and of others. It assists participants to learn to accept a range of views, while utilising the diversity to achieve optimal outcomes. OrgZoo was considered to be the best learning tool to engage participants through discussions on how to assign the right people to the right job and how to lead the team to accomplish the goal in different situations.

Who

The workshops have 50-60 participants each, comprised of people from Thailand, Cambodia, Myanmar, Malaysia, Indonesia, Bangladesh and India. So far 1000 participants have benefited from the program.

What

Many people in the Thai working environment have a fixed management style, according to their past experiences and corporate culture. The 'embracing diversity' module was designed

BECOMING ADAPTABLE

to help the participants understand human behaviours in different business and social settings. The half-day module was conducted to allow the participants to understand the types of behaviours revealed in different business settings and how to adjust them to fit various situations.

How (did OrgZoo activities help)

Team members discussed behaviours and the importance of each OrgZoo character in different situations. When presented with changed business goals or missions, the participants negotiated in collaborative teams to restructure the organisation in response to the change. Team members learned to appreciate each other's differences and how to make the best out of them amidst limitations.

Outputs (tangible short-term value delivered)

Behavioural DNA of the team — current and future (plus difference analysis).

Strategic plan to implement the changes arising from the scenario planning conversations.

Outcomes (intangible long-term value delivered)

Participants learned to understand and embrace diversity in their organisation and to see this as a strength. This program is recognised to contribute to the development of effective individual and team performance, fostering sustainable organisational growth in the long run.

2. Who becomes adaptable?

Everyone behaves, or misbehaves, depending on perspective

Behaviour, and therefore misbehaviour, is subjective. Each person has their own boundaries on how they feel they should behave. Often this is subconscious and inconsistent.

Do you sometimes look back on an event and wish you had behaved differently? The situation is not always clear at the time; after it's over, the reality of what happened seems more tangible and easier to understand. Many people struggle with how to behave in the uncertainty of the moment. It is not just about deciding to be good, whatever that means: deliberate misbehaviour is a common strategy for protesting, for example in political situations. Gandhi used the concept of civil disobedience to change social perceptions and the structure of society in South Africa (History.com editors 2010, 2021). So if we can choose behaviours sometimes, can we do it all the time?

BECOMING ADAPTABLE

The first benefit to *Becoming Adaptable* is that you get to decide and manage your own behaviour. This allows for better behavioural choices in the moment, rather than trying to recover from poor behaviour later.

A more significant benefit is being able to influence the behaviour of others — albeit carefully, ethically and respectfully. Doing this well creates benefits for activities such as community collaboration projects and criminal reform initiatives. The opposite also happens. For example, sending young offenders to prison can negatively influence their behaviours for the rest of their lives, damaging the individuals and society.

Influencing behaviour has consequences. Others may not agree with you about what's right. There is diversity within and across cultures as to what behaviour is appropriate and when. This is why facilitating such discussions works best in an inclusive way, leading with questions rather than instructions.

Consciously managing behavioural choice is a challenging task, but a highly beneficial one when you do it well. At first this seems awkward, but with practice you can become adaptable in how you interact with others. This is not trying to change your values or your personality: it's giving you the ability to choose, which in turn builds your resilience and makes you capable of dealing with a wider range of situations.

When you excel at being adaptable, you can lead others to become adaptable too. This has important ethical implications. If you choose to influence others, you accept the responsibility of helping them for their benefit and not controlling them for your own benefit.

We are human because we consciously socialise

When Descartes declared *cogito ergo sum* (*I think, therefore I am*), he was making the point that conscious awareness is essential to

2. Who becomes adaptable?

existence. There is no doubt in my mind that being human is much more than simply existing.

Plants and inanimate objects exist without evidence of thinking. Some animals think, but their level of existence is not as rich as what most humans experience or desire. Being human is special because it goes beyond this basic existence at a patterned transactional level. By this I mean that humans have flourished because of our ability to connect socially and elevate from the transactional through to transformational and sometimes into transcendent states (Bennet *et al* 2019). We have learned to collaborate in ways that other forms of life on Earth have not been able to achieve. As a result, we have come to dominate the Earth. The intangible aspects of being human — such as trust, relationships, creativity, loyalty, and caring beyond yourself — have accelerated the evolution of society and human achievement.

The highest levels of social achievement, such as space travel and humanitarian programs in disasters, are not available to all people in all places. Some people who have access to resources are not motivated to achieve. Some people cannot achieve because of health-related challenges. Some people, through no fault of their own, do not have access to the learning and resources needed to rise much above basic existence.

Unequal access to resources is one of the most complex issues facing humanity. It will require more than just thinking to resolve. In facing complex challenges, behaviour and social interactions are more likely than tangible resources to influence successful outcomes. The presence of vast differences in peoples' access to resources, either within a culture or across cultures, contributes to misunderstandings and conflict. The way we experience the world depends on the resources we expect to be available to us. We see these as our rights and the way we behave and interact with others depends on whether these rights are satisfied. The United Nations identified a set of basic human rights in the 1948 Universal Declaration of Human Rights (un.org/en/universal-declaration-

BECOMING ADAPTABLE

human-rights). More than 70 years later those rights are not yet consistently available to everybody, everywhere. Differences in behaviour, social expectations, and political manoeuvring have a lot to do with our limited progress on human rights.

So, how does all this relate to behavioural adaptability?

The way you behave depends on how you perceive the situations you face. If you accept a situation as fair and reasonable, you engage with the flow of events and feel a sense of identity in the society. If you perceive that the situation is not acceptable, you reject the system and try to make changes.

In any group, some people will be happy with the current situation and some will not. Some will believe they are being taken advantage of, leading to conflict. The situation can rapidly evolve into a negative spiral of warring parties engaging in attack and counterattack. Some well-meaning people might try to help others whom they see as less fortunate than themselves. This offer of assistance may be accepted or perceived as inappropriate interference. The body of literature on 'White saviour complex' shows that the views from the various positions can be wildly different. Responding to this kind of situation is not about who is right and who is wrong. Both parties may have points of justification for their perspective. It is a matter of approaching the differences in a way that generates understanding rather than conflict.

Understanding what others think about you and your motives is challenging to assess objectively. It takes a lot of inquiry and open conversation to understand where a person with vastly different life experiences is coming from. I have experienced this first-hand. I volunteer in a community whose aim is to listen to what minority groups desire and then engage with them in actions to achieve what they say they need. In this community, diversity is respected and all people are considered as valued and contributing members of society. The arrangements are inclusive to enable collaborative programs that the members themselves highlight as priorities. The

2. Who becomes adaptable?

approach is relationship-based, recognising the value of diversity in society. It seeks to engage members and connect across community groups.

This is a different perspective from traditional welfare models which are based on a problem mindset; that is, their purpose is to fix the problems of underprivileged people who need help. This mindset leads to perceiving different approaches as 'alternative' and not worth taking seriously. This limits what can be achieved for the communities involved. Do-gooders who think they know what others want or need are often misinformed by their own judgement and perspective. The biggest cause of these misunderstandings is the tendency to assume, determine and tell, instead of asking, listening and collaborating as partners.

Being different is a challenging road to take, as is accepting that differences in others are as valid as your own. Even if your ideas seem necessary and logical, they may not get the support required to turn them into reality. I believe there is a huge need for behavioural adaptability and stronger connections between the peoples of the world. However, there is little demand to act on this. Some people deny there is a problem; some do not see behaviour as part of the possible solution; and others are just not interested.

This book offers ways to bridge the gaps in how we work to create collaborative partnerships and work towards common goals. Achieving positive impact is more likely when we take what exists now and tweak elements of it towards cocreation of better options. This evolutionary approach is more achievable than trying to completely change the whole system. To implement it, we must focus on doing what we can, instead of arguing about what we cannot do.

Everyone is a stakeholder of your behaviour

The point of this chapter is to acknowledge that how you behave affects yourself and everyone you interact with.

BECOMING ADAPTABLE

The way you behave, ideally the way you *choose* to behave, influences everything in your life. This includes who is drawn to you and who chooses to disconnect, the opportunities you attract and the challenges you face.

The world is unfair. People who behave amazingly well do not always get what they deserve, and some poorly-behaved people get more. Regardless, we all benefit from becoming more adaptable and gaining the resilience and confidence to cope with unfairness. Some of us will find the courage to try to realign the world's imbalance.

Of course, there are people who knowingly choose to behave in ways that are inappropriate, such as criminal and unethical behaviour. We like to think they get the punishment they are due, but this does not always happen. Although the world is a wonderful place, it has faults. Many of those faults are caused by inappropriate behaviours. The more we can understand behaviour and learn to make conscious choices about how to behave across a range of contexts, the more likely we are to achieve our goals.

SUCCESS STORY
Observing group dynamics through the lens of OrgZoo

Nicole Stoeker and Peter Renner
OZAN Ambassadors, Switzerland

Context (where and when)

During the coronavirus crisis, Zurich airport had little air traffic. Airport management decided to use airport staff to assist with contact tracing to fight the pandemic. I was working as a part-time member of this team.

Why?

Airport employees needed to adjust their activities and behaviours to address the immediacy of the pandemic. One barrier was the relatively low level of capabilities to address the tasks at hand.

Who?

Many of the repurposed people had performed routines tasks and had low experiences and skills in the new requirements. Most of them typically displayed Ant behaviours to address these routine tasks. One particular challenge was the poor computer skills. I offered to teach them computer basics, which they were interested in. I wrote a concept, presented it to our management and got permission to proceed. Participants voluntarily attended and were motivated to learn.

What?

The first class was all women over 50 years old. The atmosphere was harmonious, gentle, and caring for each other. I knew and liked most of them.

We had a positive start and shared experiences during the breaks. I observed a shift in their behaviour from the perception of formal learning environment to these informal interactions.

BECOMING ADAPTABLE

They forgot about their Ant behaviour and acted like young Bees, willing to learn new skills. They were curious like Kids who wanted to grow. In the end they were incredibly happy and thankful. I felt like an Owl, grateful that I could support all of them.

The second group was totally different: men and women from around 40 to 55 years old, from different shifts. I was not sure whether they knew each other well or not and I only knew some of them. The behaviours and computer skills were quite different. These ranged from not knowing how to hold a mouse, up to a good understanding of computer work. It was a challenge to satisfy all of them because to the diversity of capabilities.

The behaviour during the break is always a good measure for the level of satisfaction in the group. There were access restrictions to different areas, making free flow a challenge. In order to re-enter the building after the coffee break, somebody had to operate the door to let people through. The smokers wanted to go outside for a cigarette. Unfortunately, this was another door on the other side of the floor. As I felt responsible for the whole group, I attempted to rush from one door to the other, ensuring everyone was able to access what they wanted. I had no chance for my own break. Nobody had an impulse to support me or to bring me something from the coffee corner.

Outputs (tangible short-term value delivered)

The airport has a significant number of people with basic computer skills and this has increased productivity and quality of work. This has assisted in the efficiency of the contract tracing activities and no doubt will assist them to perform better when they return to their normal roles after the pandemic. This investment in training was a good use of resources at a time when there was little else they could be doing.

Outcomes (intangible long-term value delivered)

My learnings from the second class? If I do not want to sacrifice my break I have to delegate like an Eagle. I am better to lead them to collaborate rather than fall into my preferred role as an Owl. The participants naturally split in small groups who were only interested in their own needs like Hyenas. At least they also were motivated like Kids in the learning program.

During the break, one of my students and co-workers stayed in the classroom playing with her mobile. My impression was that she was introverted, keeping distance and being incredibly quiet. As I like to play around with the Zoo metaphors like a Gibbon, I checked out how I could engage her more. She had a t-shirt with the motif "I don't need therapy, I just need to go skiing." I used this as an entry point and asked her whether this was true. Soon I had found her favourite topic and we had a good time together. I changed my opinion about her and found her much more positive and engaged after the connection was made.

Despite the differences both classes were satisfied with the learning. When they left the room they gave me positive feedback. They acknowledged that I was patient with them and also experienced with teaching and computers. Two days later, I met one of the students on the floor and she told me that she had just passed a test with the best grade ever. Prior to that she had struggled because she could not use the computer well enough. The sense of achievement in her appealed to my preferred behaviours of Quercus robur and Owl.

Receiving feedback was a big gift for me and helped to build my confidence. Now I have some fans at work and I keep supporting and building on our relationships whenever we meet.

To hold this group energy, making sure that everybody felt comfortable, and to serve all the different levels of learning, was exhausting. I found that having the OrgZoo metaphors enabled me to adapt my own behaviours and better understand the behavioural dynamics of others. I was able to deliver a better quality learning experience for the participants and feel proud that I made a difference for them. Reflecting on the challenges, I admire teachers who do this all the time.

BECOMING ADAPTABLE

3. What is achieved by being adaptable?

Being adaptable builds resilience and sustainability, reduces stress and enhances performance (McKeown 2012). Research into adaptability has significantly increased in the last decade, largely as it has become recognised as a positive characteristic for dealing with the complexities of the modern world (Chan 2014).

Adaptability has long been acknowledged as a survival mechanism. This is highlighted in the quote widely attributed to Charles Darwin: "It is not the strongest of the species that survives, nor the most intelligent that survives. It is the one most adaptable to change." It was actually a professor of management who said this in 1963 when explaining the importance of Darwin's work. Although Darwin never said it, the truism remains valid in personal and professional life. (Anonymous 2016, 2020)

Dealing constructively with change could involve identifying a better range of options when reacting to unexpected circumstances, or deliberately altering the direction of your life or industry. When Cirque du Soleil recruit their performers, they start with talented

BECOMING ADAPTABLE

athletes and gymnasts and challenge them with three words. They ask:

— Are you *curious* enough to explore something different?
— Do you have the *courage* to commit to this change?
— Are you *adaptable* enough to succeed?

In many fields career progression has all but been replaced by career change. People change jobs more often, they move through industries and geographies multiple times during their professional life. We are not moving away from traditional careers: we have already moved. Redundancy of jobs in traditional fields is common and completely new roles are emerging in many places. The structure of large organisations is decentralising and becoming more networked, with fuzzy boundaries. In these contexts adaptability is critical to success for individuals, organisations, societies and cultures.

If adaptability has always been important, aren't we doing it already? The short answer is yes, but too few people are adapting quickly enough to changed conditions. Some people are highly adaptable and they are leveraging this capability to become leaders in their chosen fields — in commercial organisations, government agencies, as entrepreneurs — or, more likely, as activists or advocates in change networks. There are many conversations around what needs to change and why, but relatively few result in actions to implement the changes. The climate change movement is one example of this. Despite all the awareness-raising and compelling evidence of looming disaster, climate deterioration and species loss are happening faster than any action that can slow, stop or reverse the impact. Whether it is Al Gore talking about climate change (climaterealityproject.org), Kate Raworth passionately highlighting the boundaries of the doughnut economy (kateraworth.com/doughnut), or the many advocates of the Pachamama Alliance sharing how to embed sustainable practices (pachamama.org/about), we are still going backwards. We need to adapt faster if we

3. What is achieved by being adaptable?

are to return to a harmonious state or, better, move into a proactive, positive ecosystem. Why is there apparently little collaboration between such organisations to generate synergies and amplify each other's programs? There is so much powerfully positive potential in these programs that is not being realised into social value. Much could be achieved if we were more adaptable and open to collaboration in networks of associations rather than hierarchies.

Why is it that these amazing social programs are not delivering the amount of change that's needed? The short answer to this complex question is two common human weaknesses:

— Believing something plausible is too easy

— Changing behaviour to adapt to a different belief is too hard

There is a big gap between believing something to be true and knowing for sure. Deepening your reflections and increasing social conversations helps to address the first challenge (what to believe and why). Further, knowing your desired outcomes is a long way from implementing the behaviours and actions required to achieve them. Committing to behavioural adaptability can accelerate what you achieve in collaboration with others as you close the gap between knowing what to do and actually doing it.

Critical thinking and complex problem-solving regularly appear on the World Economic Forum's list of essential future skills. With critical thinking we reflect on what we are told before we simply believe it. This is necessary because people who wish to influence you know how to make their message believable: good messages support positive social outcomes; and bad messages take advantage of your good will to exploit you or others. We are so bombarded with messages that it is hard to sort the good from the bad (acknowledging that each individual will have a different opinion on where the boundary lies). This is an inevitable outcome of relentless consumerism.

BECOMING ADAPTABLE

We are subconsciously wired to preserve our safe steady state. The normal brain is naturally risk-averse and pattern-oriented, and this is reinforced by the structures embedded in society and culture. This reduces our adaptability over time, to the point that behaving differently seems like a risk. Significant momentum and social pressure are needed to persuade someone to change their behaviour. In a constantly changing world, staying the same soon makes you irrelevant. When marketing messages play on a fear of missing out (FOMO), it is hard to know who is genuinely trying to help you and who is trying to manipulate you for their own benefit.

There is a cost-free alternative. You can develop your own behavioural adaptability, enabling you to change in a way that you determine is your best way forward. This requires effort, but you are in charge of your own destiny. You are more likely succeed if you commit to this with a like-minded community. Being human means (for most of us) that we are social creatures who are more engaged in quests if we do them with others. This works in small teams and in larger organisations. The World Economic Forum recently (August 2020) released a report arguing that successful future organisations will be more socially responsible and operate through ecosystems more than hierarchies.

As Kate Raworthy eloquently points out, this necessarily involves a change of mindset and a change of behaviour. The so-called four A's (Shelley 2017) provide a sequential process for achieving this:

1. Awareness: a shift in your 'knowing'
2. Attitude: a shift in your mindset, intent and behaviour
3. Ability: a shift in your capability to implement actions to achieve the desired outcomes
4. Action: the effective implementation of the actions to realise the benefits

It is important to do the steps in order shown. Step 1 creates *awareness*, a necessary foundation of any constructive path forward. You need to truly understand the fundamental issues, complexities,

3. What is achieved by being adaptable?

and interdependent aspects of the situation; to understand the situation as a whole system with a wide spectrum of stakeholders, not as an isolated initiative. Once participants have a deep knowledge of the whole challenge from a systems thinking perspective, the natural response is to resist moving forward. Many people do not like to engage in complex change because it involves making decisions in uncertainty. Remember: uncertainty and risk exist in everything we do, in social human systems and in natural environments.

Step 2 addresses some of these uncertainties to build an *attitude* of support. It involves engaging people in conversations that reduce resistance and build engagement. The facilitator uses questions to shift participants' mindset from resistance to engagement. This is achieved by collectively answering concerns and by building contingencies to manage possible risks.

Once people are aware and engaged, they often realise that they want to commit to the changes but are not sure how to do that. Step 3, *ability*, facilitates conversations about what resources and capabilities will be needed to achieve success. This may involve education, training, finance, political influence, communications, wider stakeholder engagement, and consideration of the time required to achieve the changes. Typically a strategy and detailed plan, with committed resources to implement, is the output of this stage. Securing agreement on this prepares the team to achieve the benefits via an Agile-style plan (agilemanifesto.org).

Step 4, *action*, implements the plan in an Agile-style development and communicates the outcomes to all stakeholders.

Although Agile was originally devised for software development, the principles with a little adjustment are consistent with most projects in complex systems, the main aspects being:

— a focus on outcomes and stakeholders

— collaborative face-to-face conversations where possible

BECOMING ADAPTABLE

- fast, iterative development cycles to demonstrate and measure progress
- embedding learning from prior cycles into design as the process proceeds

The final item in the principles of the original Agile manifesto (agilemanifesto.org/principles.html) proposes that "At regular intervals, the team reflects on how to become more effective, then tunes and adjusts its behaviour accordingly." This creates an applied social learning ecosystem (Shelley and Goodwin 2018) to optimise learning for those involved in creating the tangible deliverables of a project.

Interactive social learning to cocreate value and build relationships

A strong theme throughout this book is the importance of creating an engaging environment for people to interact with each other in a constructive manner. This is consistent with other modern approaches such as Agile, design thinking, student-centred learning, complex problem-solving, cocreation, and distributed leadership.

Success in all these approaches relies on relationships, as manifested in the behaviours displayed in context by each of the participants. The behaviours required during a brainstorming session are very different from what is optimal for a prioritisation session. It is not possible to describe an overall set of behaviours that characterise a successful team. We can, however, ask the team what they believe is the best behavioural profile for them in a given situation. This is simple and quick to generate using the OrgZoo Behavioural DNA activity (see chapter 7).

Once a team builds trusted relationships, the ecosystem becomes self-organising. The flow of knowledge and insights accelerates and this stimulates synergies between team members. Each person acts as a catalyst of the others' thoughts, and this generates new

3. What is achieved by being adaptable?

knowledge. The team becomes a highly adaptable and energised environment that can cocreate options for previously unknown challenges. Such inclusive social learning ecosystems are exciting to be part of, as they attract the very best of people and encourage them to exercise extreme adaptability.

Why games work

Games are a common way of interacting in applied social learning ecosystems and Agile design labs.

Well-designed games are effective because they are creative, inclusive and fun to play. Children learn extremely fast through play, and recently gamification and serious play have become extremely popular for rapid adult learning in professional and educational fields. Apps for gamified learning and quizzes aim to make learning more interesting, engaging and measurable. These have become a normal part of formal education as well as professional development (Allen and Sutton 2019).

Games enable a range of behaviours to be applied. People enjoy exploring and discovering, but do not enjoy just listening to facts or being told rigid answers. Clever game design leverages psychology and typical patterned behaviour to motivate players to engage in the activities. Games allow rapid learning from failure in a safe environment. The risks are low and the insights repeatable, encouraging people to build intangible capabilities like confidence, acting outside their normal comfort zone, and *Becoming Adaptable*. Part of this development experience is a growing ability to 'read the room.' The more experienced we become at sensemaking and reflecting in the moment, the better we get at seeing what others don't. This ability is stimulated in games and is priceless for creativity and building relationships.

OrgZoo activities from the very beginning were game-based. Even before gamification became a big trend, OrgZoo activities were designed as inclusive, cocreative activities that participants play to

BECOMING ADAPTABLE

generate an undefined set of possibilities, rather than to arrive at a predefined answer. The socialisation of possibilities across a diversity of participants, to share insights from different perspectives and then reflect on their relative merits, is standard in OrgZoo games. These have developed over the past two decades into a comprehensive set of sophisticated activities for professional and organisational development, and yet still appear like games to the participants. OrgZoo activities are detailed in Chapters 6 and 7.

Fun-damentals

A former student, Chinmay Ananda, and I shared a habit of making up and playing with words. We remained in touch after he graduated, and I was delighted when he titled his first book *FUNdamentals of Financial Statements* (2016). Aware of finance's drab reputation, he was trying to show that finance could be fun as well as profitable.

Although this was mainly a marketing tactic, it makes an important point about engaging people in what you are sharing. The fun element of OrgZoo games is a critical part of their success. If people are enjoying themselves, they are more confident and open-minded. This puts their brain into a divergent mindset and stimulates creativity.

So 'fun-damental' is not just a pun on words: it highlights an expected mindset and associated behaviours to invest in so that you get the most from your interactions with other participants.

This chapter connects multiple aspects of why behavioural adaptability is important and shows how behaviour can accelerate or prevent progress. This is the high-level fun chapter and, of course, the devil is in the detail (Chapters 6 and 7).

Fun, inclusivity, humour, socialisation and optimism are all fundamental to getting positive outcomes from facilitated activities. The aim is

3. What is achieved by being adaptable?

to engage a group of participants in sharing their insights and generating value collectively.

Excellent facilitation may look simple and easy to replicate. Remember: looks are deceptive. Expert facilitation is not a formula; it is a creative improvisation that is inclusive of everyone in the room. It is a complex creative expression akin to a conductor leading an orchestra through the performance of a piece of music as it is being written.

> *"Intelligence is the ability to adapt to change."*
> *— Stephen Hawking*

BECOMING ADAPTABLE

SUCCESS STORY
Harmonising collaboration and competition to increase sales

Elena Denisova and Vadim Shiryaev
OrgZoo Ambassadors, Moscow

Context (where and when)

An international food retailing company operating over 10,000 outlets across 45 countries had some challenges in their sales growth in Moscow. Internal competition among their staff was slowing the growth of sales. Management and employees from different outlets had different opinions on the best way forward and this was causing internal conflict about the organisation's main goals and final results.

Why?

Despite having the appropriate resources in place, sales were falling and the number of regular customers declining. There was a business imperative to turn the business's profitability around in outlets across Moscow and the region.

Who?

Team members from a cross-section of outlets and levels in the organisation were gathered to participate in workshops to discuss the challenges. These represented frontline customer services, outlet managers, marketers and a human resource specialist. The main objectives were the alignment of individual goals with the overall goal of the company and to discuss a common understanding of the culture and behaviour required for them to improve.

What?

The workshop was facilitated to provide the opportunity for all participants to express their views on the problem and then collaborate to create solutions to consider. The participants used OrgZoo to understand the nature of collaborative and competitive behaviours and how these need to be addressed in different ways. An initiative was created to collaborate internally to become more competitive externally. Within each outlet employees focused on behaviours that generated better customer service and presented a friendly atmosphere in the store. There were synergies across the outlets as there was greater awareness from a common campaign.

How? (did OrgZoo activities help)

OrgZoo practitioners firstly facilitated an OrgZoo icebreaker to familiarise the participants with the characters and the concept of behavioural adaptability. They then facilitated Behavioural DNA of collaboration, competition and customer service to increase the awareness of their impacts among employees across the entire organisation. A campaign built around appropriate behaviour was then implemented across all outlets and sales impacts were measured by store.

Outputs (tangible short-term value delivered)

There was a significant increase in sales during the campaign, attributed to the more appropriate behaviours being implemented. It is expected that customer loyalty will be positively impacted.

Outcomes (intangible long-term value delivered)

Employees have begun to interact better and collaboration increased. They each took more individual and collective responsibility for performance, offered solutions and implemented them in practice.

Management has begun to trust employees, to listen to their opinion and support ideas flowing form the frontline customer services to generate ongoing improvements.

Employee engagement and productivity has improved because they saw that they were heard, and their opinion was important, and valuable, to the company. The business owner was convinced that an effective collaborative approach has a positive impact on business competitiveness.

BECOMING ADAPTABLE

4. When should we facilitate adaptability development?

You may have noticed that first chapters in this book are questions posed in the same order as depicted in Figure 4.1. The case summaries shared by OZAN Ambassadors are presented in the same format. This is no accident.

These questions — why, who, what, when and where — will guide you towards success in almost any endeavour.

It is critical to start with *why*, to be sure that you are committed to the activities you are about to embark upon (Sinek 2011).

Next, pay attention to *who* is involved. Left to yourself, you may have an answer, maybe even a few options for how to proceed. With multiple people sharing a diversity of experiences, insights and perspectives, there are many more options available to select from — or to hybridise into something new.

Once you know what value you are creating and *why*, with guidance from the aligned perspectives of the right people in the conversation (*who*), then *what* to do becomes easy to determine.

BECOMING ADAPTABLE

By the time you ask *when*, your knowledge of *why*, *who* and *what* should be well advanced and the direction clearly understood by all.

What happens when you decide to do something without the benefit of all the prior conversations? You announce your intent (*what* to do, and *when*) and the questions just start rolling in. *Why* are you doing this, *who* is involved, did you ask Expert A or Leader B? I remember working with a community leader who would always ask, "Have you bounced your proposal off the community members yet? If not, why are you bringing it to me? It is clearly not ready!"

When is important, but is a late-maturing question best addressed after other details are known. Sometimes the question of *when* deserves to be rushed, for example in emergencies. In such instances you may not know all the details necessary to make optimal decisions, and you can deal with the consequences of that later. Away from emergency situations, it is best to hold *when* as the pivot point between planning (*why*, *who* and *what*) and action (*how*). How we implement something is heavily dependent on when it is needed.

Think about all those assignments you did in your formal education. If you invested effort every week leading up to the deadline, you would turn in a beautiful piece of work that truly represented your talent and knowledge. However, life often gets in the way of such strategic dedication, and you end up rushing to finish the assignment at the last minute. The quality and scope of the project suffers because the *when* question was not answered at the appropriate pivot point.

Becoming Adaptable is like a learning assignment. If you practise over a longer timeframe and reflect on progress as you go, you develop more mature capabilities and a wider scope of behaviours. Under pressure you will be more confident, experienced and capable of adapting to the needs of the moment

4. When should we facilitate adaptability development?

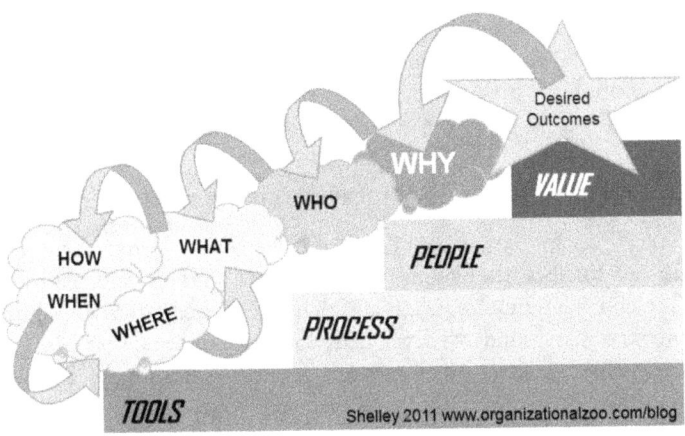

Figure 4.1. Optimal order of questions in designing initiatives

Attending a weekend intensive learning unit may be convenient, but it does not give the depth of experience required to develop and practise the skills at a level that amplifies success. One of my daughters said to me, when she was a teenager, "Oh come on Dad, not everything in life is a learning experience!" To which I calmly responded, "Of course it is." Repeated practice over time approaches perfection.

The simple answer to when to become adaptable is — always. Live with it embedded into every moment of every day.

— Before you meet others, consider a range of ways to behave

— While you are with others, remain alert to how things are happening; perhaps start planning how to adapt your behaviour to optimise outcomes.

— After an event, reflect on what else you could have done to prepare; use this insight in planning for the next interaction.

BECOMING ADAPTABLE

This pattern of reflecting before, during and after activities is fundamental to being a reflective practitioner (Schön 1983). The descriptions of how to facilitate activities in Chapter 7 reflect this cycle of *prepare before*, *implement flexibly*, and *reflect after*.

When is an OrgZoo interaction most effective?

Everything humans do is influenced by behaviour. When things do not go to plan, the failure often relates to misaligned behaviour. OrgZoo is a quick, engaging and rich way to facilitate meaningful interactions around whatever behaviour-related topic you wish to explore. As unique situations arise, a creative facilitator can find ways to use OrgZoo to initiate a relevant conversation that elicits new possibilities.

Part of the magic of the OrgZoo experience is that the more diverse the participants, the richer the conversations become. This is because the wider range of perspectives provides for more differences to discuss. Participants generate insights by exploring these differences. Most people are more patterned than they realise: our own culture feels familiar and natural. The OrgZoo games allow participants to quickly adopt and accept other ways of thinking. This is a significant step in developing awareness of your own behavioural capabilities.

When somebody suggests alternative behaviours, most people will initially reject or at least withdraw somewhat. Taking a less direct path, OrgZoo activities encourage participants to safely explore a range of behaviours. Through these safe conversations, people soon realise their own preferred way is quite limited compared with the full range of possibilities. This is a common experience in OrgZoo conversations, which deliberately nudge people out of their comfort zones. In the safe environment of an OrgZoo interaction, individuals can explore alternatives deeply with others without feeling overwhelmed or threatened.

4. When should we facilitate adaptability development?

The OrgZoo character set provides a politically neutral language to explore the behaviours as separate entities from the people displaying them. In research using OrgZoo characters to understand team dynamics, participants saw the characters as a shared creative language (Shelley 2012). This narrows the gap when some participants are using their second or third language. By speaking about the characters rather than the people displaying the behaviours, it is possible to depersonalise the conversation and understand the behavioural dynamics and their effects, separately from the people.

The power of OrgZoo is that people from all cultures can recognise a behaviour as the same thing while disagreeing about the acceptability of that behaviour. For example, Lion is universally recognised as strong control-and-command behaviour. In hierarchical cultures of Asia and the Middle East this is perceived as a positive characteristic, especially for leadership. In more individualistic Western cultures, Lion's strong command-and-control is cherished by some senior leaders and perceived by others as micromanagement. When facilitating Behavioural DNA (see Chapter 7) with young adults in Australia, England, USA and Canada I have seen a distinct disliking of this behaviour in many contexts. OrgZoo activities thus reveal insights about the desirability of individual behaviours in different contexts and cultures. These dialogues enable all participants to acknowledge that there is no clearly right or wrong behaviour: what matters is the cultural expectation in context. Once people realise this, the conversations become rich and powerful for personal and professional development.

National, ethic and organisational cultures do not necessarily reflect any specific individual within them. Stereotypes are dangerous because they represent high-level patterns across a group. Individuals within a culture can be typical of those patterns — or they can be vastly different. This is why OrgZoo activities are usually done at two levels, first in small groups and subsequently by comparison

BECOMING ADAPTABLE

across groups. Participants are encouraged to look for patterns of similarity and difference at both levels.

The mythical character of Dragon highlights the difference between individual perspectives and stereotypical patterns of interpretation across cultures. Dragon is a whole animal capable of displaying many behaviours; unlike the OrgZoo characters, it is not a metaphor for an individual behaviour. In most Western myths, the dragon is an evil character to be feared, a vicious fire-breathing demon to be fought and conquered.

In Eastern cultures the dragon is presented as a nurturing creature who is a protector of the people and environment. Typically, the Eastern dragon is revered and people desire to be like them. A dragon in a Western children's story is mostly slain by the human hero character; the Eastern dragon is the hero of the story.

Figure 4.2. Western dragon   *Figure 4.3. Eastern dragon*

The Dragon character reminds us to consider the individual behaviours, not the whole person, when making decisions about behavioural interactions. The OrgZoo characters are carefully chosen to avoid such cultural biases.

4. When should we facilitate adaptability development?

Questions around cultural stereotypes are inevitable and must be treated with respect. They are part of the learning process of *Becoming Adaptable*. They pop out early. I have been asked in the Middle East where is the camel; and in Scandinavia why there is no wolf. People in African nations are pretty happy as the OrgZoo contains quite a few of their iconic animals, although some of the made-up characters can stimulate some fun dialogue too.

The best way to answer the question is with a return question: what behaviour does the camel, wolf, or other suggested character represent? Usually this stimulates a conversation that highlights many different perceptions. This reinforces the point that just because something is an icon in a country, it does not represent an adequately consistent behaviour that makes it usable across cultures. These conversations are not disruptive; they are informative and should be encouraged. In the end it is about encouraging questions and sharing perspectives. If the facilitator is a role model for this, they are more effective in accelerating the journey of *Becoming Adaptable* for their participants.

Having been tested hundreds of times in many cultural groups, mostly the OrgZoo characters are quite universally recognisable. However, the approach is a creative metaphor, so please do not apply strict logic or, worse, use it to categorise someone! This must never be done. The OrgZoo can be used to highlight that a person may be displaying a behaviour in a specific situation, but not applied like an overall stereotype of personality.

Differences in perspective underline the flexibility that humans demonstrate in their behaviour. When we understand this is normal, we can ourselves become more adaptable in the way we choose to behave.

BECOMING ADAPTABLE

SUCCESS STORY
Working with change — a Hong Kong example

Laurel Sutton
OZAN Ambassador, Australia

Why?

Change is constant. For some organisations and individuals change is unsettling and creates problems in working productively and working together. In this particular instance, change had become almost a way of life and, whilst it was accepted it would happen frequently, it was nonetheless difficult for people to cope with. Coping strategies needed to be developed for individuals and teams to manage and cope with change, and to promote harmony which was identified as important from a Hong Kong perspective.

Who?

The people involved were from a Hong Kong organisation involved in tertiary education. All participants were staff from various areas, with the vast majority being teaching staff. Others were administrative support staff or managers from the various areas, so all levels were represented and engaged in the workshop.

What?

A Hong Kong tertiary organisation had been undergoing constant change. The change was imposed with staff having no alternative except to accept it. Often it was a change in procedures and methods of operating, which created instability and a sense of uncertainty. Some were constantly reverting to previous ways of doing things, which was creating a problem for team leaders. There was also a sense of disharmony and some conflict, which was unacceptable. The leaders were being held to account for the disharmony. People wanted to work together and have a harmonious workplace, as this is what was valued by them as individuals and the organisation. The staff were puzzled by the behaviours they were seeing and experiencing, and were wanting to understand them and to be able to guide people towards working together again and working with the changes.

The heads of one department thought the issue important enough to free people of their work commitments for one day and to bring them together in a workshop: to try to understand what was happening; and to develop alternative ways of behaving in the face of change.

How? (did OrgZoo activities help)

Prior to the workshop the participants were asked to respond to a scenario that was codesigned with the heads of the department. As part of the response, they were encouraged to reflect on their own behaviour and complete the personal profile using the Organizational Zoo profiler on the website. Bringing the generated profile to the workshop created a baseline for people to look at their own behaviours, as well as introducing them to the concept of the OrgZoo.

The workshop was highly interactive and activity-based. It used Elisabeth Kubler Ross's 'seven stages of change' model to understand the phases of change. The OrgZoo cards were used to look at and understand behaviours associated with each phase.

Once the phase of integration was reached, the cards and animal metaphors were used to identify core/accepted behaviours, desired/accepted behaviours, and not-tolerated behaviours. A reflective exercise using the personal profiles and the discoveries from the workshop was facilitated so that people could think about behaviours they might need to take responsibility for changing in themselves. And to better understand how leaders might facilitate these behaviours, the

BECOMING ADAPTABLE

Invisible Maze was used and processed using the animal metaphors for behaviour again.

Follow-up to the workshop was provided by the facilitator through "Notes for Taking Action" which included reflective questions and copies of the profiles for the organisation that the workshop generated. The group were highly energetic, positive and playful, which assisted with the learning and the acceptance of the process and outcomes.

Outputs (tangible short-term value delivered)

Four weeks later the group were asked to share a story about how they had used the learnings from the workshop and what impact they had.

Here are some responses:

— *"From the OrgZoo workshop, I have learnt that if I want to get closer to a friend/colleague, I need to understand more about him/her. I could invite him/her to do the online exercise and create a behaviour profile if possible or observing which kinds of animal they are more like to be. I may then learn more about their behaviours, attitude and working style."*

— *"If I am not sharing the same or similar behaviours with my friend/colleague, I have to adjust my style or tone in order to put myself into his/her shoes. This may enhance the effectiveness of our communication. After building the rapport, I will be able to help him/her or work together with him/her smoothly and in good mood."*

— *"Recently, I have spoken more actively with my neighbours in the lift of the mansion where I live and tried to infer which animals they were likely to be. I then talked with them, starting from their interested topics next time when I met them, and we have entered happy conversations shortly. Thankfully, I found myself was getting closer to them."*

5. Where does behavioural adaptability apply to success?

In the past, most people became more patterned as they aged. Careers progressed relatively slowly, mostly upwards in a structured hierarchy, and people tended to remain in the same industry. Their patterns of behaviour and ways of thinking became more rigid through repeated, similar experiences. Career paths encouraged specialisation; acquiring that deeper expertise came at the cost of a narrowed scope of interests. There were generalists too, though their numbers were smaller and they were outside the mainstream career paths. In a world with stable and predictable patterns, *Becoming Adaptable* is the reverse of how most people progress through life.

Over the past couple of decades, change has progressively happened more quickly. In this new world, people need to adapt their knowledge and skills, keep their options open, and be prepared for significant changes in career pathways and personal lifestyle choices that are outside their own control. People cannot rely on developing a sense of stability in this new world. In some countries more than half the workforce is now contracted rather than salaried, making

BECOMING ADAPTABLE

knowledge and capability building less of an investment for organisations. Restructures are common, so even experienced people can be dealt sudden and unexpected changes. Workers cannot ever quite fully relax into what previously would have been considered permanent employment. The phrase 'settle down' is almost redundant.

Retraining can prepare people with skills for new roles and industries. Changing behaviour to fit new expectations and workplace cultures is less straightforward.

Some people are rightfully admired for consistently saying and doing the right thing across a wide range of situations and with a diversity of people. Other people seem rigid and struggle to interact positively with people different from themselves. They may be highly skilled in a particular field, but not so good with other people. For some people a highly adaptable style is a natural talent; for some it is a deliberately learned behaviour; and for others adaptability is limited.

Almost all senior public figures are now trained in behaviour and communication skills. For example, if you closely watch a politician engaging with the media, you can see when they are within their comfort zone. Equally, it is clear when they are following the advice of their media coach but acting outside their comfortable range. Journalists and interviewers are well versed in such skills and will behave in a way that is more likely to secure their story. They can charm an unsuspecting interviewee into sharing something they should not have, or they can aggressively provoke. This behavioural tango is entertaining for avid people-watchers, although challenging for the people involved. In our highly connected and competitive world, a behavioural slip can be costly, including job and reputation loss. An error of judgement can almost immediately be shared everywhere within minutes.

5. Where does behavioural adaptability apply to success?

I believe risk aversion and anxiety levels are higher in the modern world because of these factors. It is not just senior people in government and organisations that feel exposed in today's volatile, uncertain, complex and ambiguous (VUCA) environment (Fuchs *et al* 2019). Everyone's behaviours are more visible by more people than ever before. The average time on internet-connected devices is high in most countries and this exposes us to a plethora of people and situations, with sometimes little or no understanding of their intent. Generally you will have some knowledge about the people you interact with in person; on the other hand, internet interactions can be almost blind. You may not know how many people are involved and may not know them all (or that they are who they say they are). We are losing control over who can access and use our information, and communications via social media are prone to misinterpretation , either deliberate or in error.

The cyber world is an area in which our behaviour has not caught up with reality. What you might say or do with a 'real world friend' is fine if shared with a close friendship group. However, when the same statement or action is shared on an open internet platform, it is totally uncontrollable.

Adapting your behaviour to these new contexts requires considerable reflection and practice. Building your behavioural adaptability helps build confidence and resilience for those inevitable unpredicted situations.

Understanding the anxiety about constant change is an important starting point when coaching yourself or others to become adaptable. People resist change because they prefer to rely on what they know (providing a sense of confidence), rather than step outside their comfort zone into what they don't know. However, if they remain in the familiar patterns of their current knowledge, they soon become irrelevant. Shifting willingly outside one's comfort zone requires strong motivation, because it goes against the natural flow

BECOMING ADAPTABLE

of how most people are wired. For this reason, the environment and facilitation process are critical to success.

Any natural system falls into the lowest energy state unless there is effort invested to elevate it. This principle applies to chemistry, nuclear physics, your physical fitness and even the mess in a teenager's room. It is where the 'use it or lose it' adage comes from. Achieving a higher state of organisation or capability requires the input of energy and effort. Behavioural adaptability is the same. Once you have become aware that greater behavioural adaptability is possible, you can then apply the practice to get better over time.

Sharing these concepts will help you and those collaborating with you to understand how to accelerate progression in behavioural adaptability. Anything worthwhile takes practice over time. This is not to say that everyone has equal capacity: we are all different in our ability to develop our behavioural capabilities, but we can all achieve some change.

There are clearly significant differences in physical capabilities between people depending on height, weight, age, level of experience, and natural talent. We invest most effort in developing our natural talents. A champion track sprinter does not enter the 100 metres freestyle swimming at the Olympic Games: athletes tend to specialise because there is greater reward in doing so. We can all improve our capabilities in any pursuit with some work, should we choose to invest in that.

This is evident in careers as well. A person more comfortable in quantitative fields is attracted to numbers-driven roles such as accountancy, science, mathematics *et cetera*. Conversely, a person with strong natural creativity is attracted to more artistic or humanities roles. These are not this-or-that dichotomies. They reflect spectrums of potential. Anyone can get better at anything with practice and persistence, if they desire to do so and invest and persist. It just requires the motivation and support to act on the desire.

5. Where does behavioural adaptability apply to success?

Behavioural adaptability is the same. There is a natural spectrum of capability and willingness to change one's behaviour. Some people reject the possibility of change; some have a desire to change but don't know how; and others are actively seeking to change. *Becoming Adaptable* can help anybody in the third group, those who seek to leverage a greater range of behaviours and achieve success (whatever that means to them).

There are many situations in which being adaptable can make life better for you. Consider what you could achieve if you were more confident and resilient, more likely to experiment, less risk averse, more likely to speak up when something is wrong. Where could you be more productive, more influential, and more engaged, if you had greater scope of behavioural capabilities?

Where are behavioural patterns in big business?

How do we know what we know about how people behave? Our understanding of behaviours is mostly limited to what we observe and what we can read or watch in various media sources. Of course, these sources are biased, both by ourselves and by the people who produce them. What we could access in the past was limited, as researchers had difficulties getting access to sufficient people prepared to share their thoughts on why they behave as they do.

These research methods assume people understand their own behaviour, or that of others they observe. Data about behaviour was costly in the past and often unreliable because of the limitations in how it could be interpreted. Qualitative research in social sciences is a relatively young field (Conner 2015, 2018) and much of what is published is challenged by others in the field (Brinkmann et al 2014) because of the limitations and biases involved. People and relationships are subjective and often inconsistent, yet we benefit by understanding how they behave and why.

Despite all these limiting factors, behaviour is one of the most fundamental aspects of being human and a very significant contributor to success of any kind. How we behave is influenced by

BECOMING ADAPTABLE

many factors, some of which we do not consciously understand. Given these parameters, there is huge value in being able to analyse behaviour more deeply, whether for curiosity, social relationships, resolving conflicts, or business. People who are more behaviourally aware build stronger relationships and are more successful in personal life and business encounters (Goleman 2009).

Businesses have always tried to understand the behaviour of their customers and competitors. The deeper and more reliable their analysis, the better they can pitch their products and services to their target market. In the last two decades there has been a perfect storm of technological development that amplified the ability to predict the behaviour of consumers. Advances in the Internet of Things (IoT), artificial intelligence (AI), big data, social media applications, machine learning and mobile devices have generated huge volumes of data on how people actually behave, not just what they say they might do. Some social media companies are now assessing people's mood through facial evaluation algorithms as they engage in video conferencing. GPS monitoring of smartphones, even when they are not in use, provides what their owners are doing and with whom they are interacting. Smart home devices add to this data to paint an even more intimate portrait of your life. AI analysis of patterns, cross-matched with transactions and interactions people engage in, produces quite reliable predictions on what people are likely to do next.

This behavioural analysis creates real-time opportunities to advertise products and services in a targeted manner at the moment of a likely sale. This data is extremely valuable for the owners of the applications and platforms, and more effective for the providers of the products and services. Your behavioural patterns are now a commodity gathered and sold in real time via internet service providers. Some people like this as they can adjust what is highlighted to them; others find it invasive and are concerned about potential misuse and manipulation. We all behave differently.

5. Where does behavioural adaptability apply to success?

Businesses have moved beyond spending their marketing budgets to try to understand what their potential customers might like and paying for generic advertising that has a low success rate. They now invest in highly targeted data to shape customised offerings to people they are confident will purchase. This is quite a significant shift in how businesses operate. It also reinforces current preferences for the customer. Rather than seeing a range of possible offerings that they had not thought about, they get targeted offerings based on what the pattern-monitoring algorithms show they have thought about. The AI is great at telling you what you do, but (as yet) is not great at suggesting creative options outside your current patterns than may be even better.

Understanding behaviour and knowing what to do with it, in context, has significant benefits. It is possible that commercial enterprises and social media organisations may understand your own behaviour as well as you understand your own. Perhaps even better. For this reason, and many others, there is a strong case for understanding your own behaviour and building greater behavioural adaptability.

SUCCESS STORY
Indonesian Banking organisation

MD Indera Tasripin
OZAN Ambassador, Singapore and Indonesia

Context (where and when)

Between February 2018 and December 2019, I facilitated a series of leadership development programs based on the OrgZoo concept for a large Indonesian financial institution. Their corporate university's primary function is upskilling and developing the competencies of its archipelago-wide managers and upper management. I first introduced components of the OrgZoo as part of my leadership development program in February 2018, which led to regular workshops afterwards until December 2019. During the program we had the opportunity to incorporate OrgZoo activities with much success and terrific reception. The onset of the pandemic and travel restrictions ceased on-site training arrangements and paved the way for existing formats to be converted into virtual activities.

Why?

Securing a consistent appointment to deliver for the financial institution was an important and breakthrough achievement. I had to convince management what unique approaches I had to offer. The inclusion of the OrgZoo as an approach and framework for the leadership development, strategic communications for leaders, and digital transformation courses, was vital and crucial in anchoring the opportunity. The risk that I undertook to invest in OrgZoo was rewarded and enabled penetration into the Indonesian market with a landmark credible organisation.

Who?

Participants in the various programs included newly promoted managers, senior executives and boardroom personnel.

Participants in Strategic Communications for Leaders sessions were senior management comprising associate directors and directors. The participants came from across Indonesia's archipelago and totalled 360 across this period.

What?

The sessions designed and facilitated in the program were:

— *Re-set 4.0: Getting Leaders to be 4.0-ready* — 2 sessions. It was a timely and pertinent goal to use Behavioural DNA profiling to assess the existing leadership mindset and organisational culture. With the DNA profile of current leadership and culture generated, the session naturally progressed to determining (future) leadership and organisational culture capable of navigating vast changes brought on by the wider implications of Indonesia's Industry 4.0 roadmap and strategy. Another training subset for the session was on developing high performance workplace and teams: the visual stimulus from OrgZoo and behavioural guidelines for contextual scenarios were progressively explored to contribute to subliminal meaning-making and insight-building for participants.

— *Professional Communication Skills for Leaders* — 4 sessions. Participants comprised newly-promoted managers in three sessions and senior management of associate directors and directors. OrgZoo activities were vital in engaging the participants and allowed them to explore new perspectives and ways of communicating using the creative metaphors.

How? (did OrgZoo activities help)

For *Re-set 4.0: Getting Leaders to be 4.0-ready* we started by assessing the existing leadership mindset and organisational culture. This was followed with a strategic presentation on

BECOMING ADAPTABLE

Indonesia's Industry 4.0 roadmap and strategy outlined by Indonesia's Ministry of Trade and Industry.

In raising greater mindset and transformation awareness of directions for Industry 4.0, the participants used OrgZoo DNA profiling to determine the leadership traits essential in navigating change through the wide-implications of Industry 4.0 (future).

Another learning goal for the session was developing high performance workplace and teams. An interactive discussion was facilitated with the participants; employing one of the OrgZoo's visual stimulus, sparking online responses on optimal and counter-productive behaviours demonstrated by the OrgZoo characters. These helped us pave the way to demonstrate what are examples of high-performance teams and their antithesis.

To facilitate more specific discussion on which are desirable and non-desirable behaviours in teams, contextual scenarios were devised, such as working with cross-functional teams and building greater trust with local and remote teams.

The selection of five metaphors which contributed to positive relationship-building, and another five metaphors which jeopardised good relationships, allowed for progressive exploration of the workplace scenarios. The facilitation and design of this activity allowed participants to subliminally generate meaning-making and build insights for themselves as they discussed, negotiated and prioritised on the range of metaphor characters for the contexts explored.

For *Professional Communication Skills for Leaders,* OrgZoo character cards were strategically used as an icebreaker and as a model for how participants can use them as conversation starters in communication scenarios such as conferences and business networking. This helped them to highlight positive traits and identify behavioural barriers. OrgZoo visuals on desirable and non-desirable behaviours of teams were also employed to progressively explore varied communication scenarios such as how leaders express opinion, manage differences, and handle diversity of views and perspectives.

Sessions heavily utilised action-learning practices, devising role plays using the OrgZoo metaphors. This allowed for workplace situations characterised by spectrum of desirable and non-desirable behaviours to come to life. The non-threatening use of metaphors allowed for role plays to explore scenarios at an implicit level; allowing for tacit identification and understanding of issues and characters, essential in creating trusted and psychologically safe exploratory space for workplace issues.

Frameworks and tools from the OrgZoo, for building trusted relationships and the importance of leading versus managing, were highly constructive building blocks for our trajectory of equipping leaders with mindset, tools, techniques and experiences to become adept and competent communicators as leaders.

Outputs

Reset 4.0:

— Behavioural DNA of leaders and organisation, current and future

— Project desired behaviours for leadership and organisation

— Tangible articulation of desirable and non-desirable behaviours for workplace or teams

— Generating and articulating behaviour guidelines expected for teams and organisation

— Framework and approach: building trusted relationships and leading versus managing, to lead high performance teams, workplace and organisations

BECOMING ADAPTABLE

Professional Communication Skills for Leaders:

— Behaviour anticipation in communication scenarios (anticipation of range of behaviours through role play of 26 metaphors)

— Increasing range of behaviour adaptability for diverse communication settings

— Framework and approach: building trusted relationships and leading versus managing- approaches for leadership communication

Outcomes

Deeper understanding of behavioural dynamics across the organisation.

Stronger levels of trust in the organisation.

Deeper and more reflective conversations about behavioural and cultural impacts.

Part B

How to start becoming adaptable

BECOMING ADAPTABLE

6. How to facilitate interactions with positive impact

The OrgZoo approach to engaging interactions

Facilitation, education and training are most often delivered as the 'defined method' or as a one-way transfer of knowledge. These traditional approaches are fine if you want to know what is already known. They work less well if you want to explore something that is new, or approach a novel problem for which an answer does not yet exist.

In many real-world challenges we are interested in what the people around us think of a subjective situation. If you invest the time to explore well, it is likely you will discover there are many perspectives and beliefs among your participants. The richest learning and the most enjoyable conversations come from sharing diverse views in a constructive way (Shelley and Goodwin 2018). Cocreating new possibilities from these collective views will produce many options that can be tried in a reversal of the traditional formal learning approach (Shelley 2020b).

BECOMING ADAPTABLE

You cannot easily search the internet for cutting-edge challenges and interesting avenues of exploration. They have not yet been addressed in your context. This does not mean you need to start from nothing every time. Rather, it's a cue to quickly explore the full range of what we collectively know, then assess what can be adapted from those insights. This is best achieved by facilitating open discussions, provoked by questions, among the people in your conversation (whether that be face to face or virtual). This is the *Conversations That Matter* approach described later in this chapter. These conversations are divergent in nature, looking outwards to create new options.

During the development of your initiative, cycles of convergent and divergent conversations will open up possibilities and then prioritise them down to an achievable list of best options. These iterative cycles of conversation help to refine and improve what we can generate from the interactions. Learning is an intangible outcome of these interactions; and refined, implementable ideas are tangible outputs.

The key features of effective facilitation are:

— inclusive
— emergent
— social
— safe
— respectful
— reflective
— conversation-based

All OrgZoo interactions are facilitated this way and aligned with the principles listed later in this chapter. Depending on the desired outcomes of the individual activity in the context of the participants, facilitators generally start with divergent exploration

6. How to facilitate interactions with positive impact

of a situation or question, then follow with alternating cycles of divergent and convergent conversation to open up possibilities and remove the weaker options. (See triple loop learning in Shelley, 2017)

Great ideas are stimulated and nurtured from insights

For every PhD, there is an equal and opposite PhD! (with apologies to Isaac Newton)

Life experiences show us that a lot of what we are taught as 'fact' is really just one aspect of the full story, which itself (over time) might turn out to be incorrect. People and knowledge are deeply subjective: we believe what we emotionally connect to, and this influences our logic and what we see as credible.

This relationship between emotion, credibility and logic has been known since the time of Aristotle, based on observed behaviour (Rapp 2010). With the development of functional magnetic resonance imaging (fMRI) and neuroscience, we now have supporting evidence.

People will believe what they want to believe, and this is strongly influenced by their personal experiences and subconscious biases. We all have biases and should be more aware of them. If you know you will interpret things in a particular way, you can try to imagine other ways of seeing the situation. Even better, you might ask someone from a different background (and therefore with a different set of perspectives and biases) what they see and why. This process is known as *creative friction* (Shelley 2017).

The structure of Conversations That Matter

Conversations are the foundation of human interactions, from early sentences practiced with your parents to high-level international negotiations between governments. The natural way for humans to interact is talking.

BECOMING ADAPTABLE

Often when people are angry with each other, a severe form of punishment is not speaking: that is, removing the right to converse. Conversation is not just a way to socialise, it is fundamental to our relationships and sense of well-being. When people are isolated, such as in a major crisis like the COVID-19 pandemic, they find creative ways to engage with others to get that sense of conversation.

Conversations That Matter is a method for getting the most out of our verbal interactions. There are other useful approaches, such as aligned conversation structures: there is never just one version of a strong concept. I first defined the *Conversations That Matter* structure in a 2009 book and later with an updated visualisation in a blog post (organizationalzoo.com/conversations-that-matter). These provide more details than the basic structure described here.

Conversations That Matter should involve stakeholders as much as possible and occur in cycles of divergence and convergence (as described above).

Conversations That Matter have five primary components that serve to generate the best results: purpose; outputs; outcomes; benefits; and beneficiaries. Each of these is briefly discussed below.

Purpose: what are we trying to achieve?

If you reflect deeply on the purpose of the conversation, you can focus your attention to increase your chances of achieving what you (and others in the conversation) want. Conversations without purpose can be fun and socially engaging and this is of value. However, allowing the conversation to wander when there is a specific purpose can less productive.

Outputs: tangible things generated from the activity

Outputs are sharable, quantifiable objects, usually available immediately after the conversation and often short-term and tactical in nature. For a brainstorming (divergent) conversation the output will be a list of options. For a prioritisation (convergent) conversation the output will be a reduced list, as the brainstorm list

6. How to facilitate interactions with positive impact

from the earlier conversation will be condensed to a few best ideas to take forward. An output could be something as significant as a signature for financial support or it could be a wide range of less-significant results such as an agreement or permission to explore an option further.

Outcomes: **intangible things generated from the activity**

Outcomes are more difficult to define precisely as they are largely intangible results such as developing trust, building relationships, opening minds and being creative (or, if the conversation was poorly facilitated, the reduction of these aspects). Outcomes are more critical in the long term and more strategic in nature than outputs. They are difficult to measure accurately, but they are felt through their impact on the social, emotional or cultural aspects of how the participants interacted. For a brainstorming conversation the outcomes could be that we had a lot of fun and generated a great deal of trust. For an effective prioritisation conversation, outcomes examples include a high level of confidence in what was discussed or a calming of the anger in the community.

Benefits: the value created from the activity and the follow-up actions

There is a strong relationship between benefits, outputs and outcomes. Value from outputs and outcomes can take a range of forms. Businesses generally focus on financial value, mainly because they are profit-motivated, the benefit is immediately visible, and it is the easiest thing to measure. Intangible outcomes, such as trust and creativity, are more important in the longer term; the value these create is in ongoing relationships and reputation, which in turn generate return business and brand loyalty. In charitable, not-for-profit and social organisations, value may manifest in intangible forms such as lives saved, quality of life, services provided, sustainability, or social contribution.

BECOMING ADAPTABLE

Beneficiaries: who receives the benefits generated

This may be a specific person, organisation or community. The beneficiaries of a conversation may not always be immediately apparent. Sometimes specific beneficiaries are the focus of the conversation and the reason for it. However, beneficiaries could be serendipitous and the people receiving the value may not have been in the conversation, or considered in it.

Facilitating *Conversations That Matter* in advance of decisions or actions is an effective way to consider a range of perspectives and possibilities. This usually highlights alternative considerations, which can lead to better options. In good conversations we often generate richer insights across all five of the elements. Sometimes we realise that our original purpose is not the best way forward and we adapt our plans for better outcomes. Given the increasing diversity of societies and stakeholders, planned actions may not be of benefit to everyone affected. In particular, it's important to understand if there are negative consequences for any stakeholders, and to consider whether and how they may need to be compensated.

Designing and facilitating effective interactions

The most noble reason to facilitate conversations is to open minds and connect people to enable them to see other perspectives. This experience positions them to generate new options, to make more informed decisions and to take better actions. Learning is the most immediately visible outcome. Other generic benefits include aligning people towards a common goal, building relationships, and driving innovation.

When you engage people in these experiences, it is critical that you remain highly aware of the impact this has on participants and your own motives (and those of the others in the conversation). A facilitator has the ethical responsibility to ensure that everyone in the conversation or activity is willingly participating and the

6. How to facilitate interactions with positive impact

environment is psychologically safe. This can change in an instant, through an unexpected and unplanned statement or action, or through a deliberate attempt to subvert the purpose of the activity. The ability to read the room and manage the participants' safety is crucial for any facilitator. Simply following a recipe plan for activities is insufficient for success. It is also an excellent example of why *Becoming Adaptable* is important.

Design insights

A significant aspect of success in facilitation is the design of the activity. Conversations That Matter are a good way to approach the design of learning activities and workshops. Start by reflecting on what you wish to achieve. How will this manifest itself in terms of outputs and outcomes, what benefits will it generate and for whom? Answering these five basic questions will provide a strong foundation for the activity design. If you are designing a multi-activity workshop (or an entire curriculum program — or even an event), make sure that the activities throughout the program flow in a meaningful way. The outputs and outcomes of one activity lead into the next activities, to reinforce the learning and build upon the new insights. This maximises the learning from the program as a whole and increase the likelihood of the new capabilities being used beyond the formal program in the workplace.

The best learning is not just about transferring existing knowledge (as most often happens in traditional formal education and training). The most important aspect of facilitating learning is the participants learning how to learn. The world is becoming increasingly unstructured and being able to makes sense of situations is a valuable capability, as is cocreating the best options with what you have in the moment. This is where existing knowledge and theories can impede progress as they are too structured to enable agile actions to proceed. In complex situations,

BECOMING ADAPTABLE

it is better to try something, see what happens, and learn from that to inform the next actions. Too much procrastination in a volatile situation can be more damaging than acting on a guess, informed by sensemaking (Snowden and Boone 2007).

A generic design approach for facilitated activities is described below. Please remember that design is a plan! it sometimes needs to be adapted, depending on where the conversations flow and how the relationships between participants and contexts emerge. However, at the same time, conversations should not be allowed to completely wander in a direction that is not aligned with the purpose of the conversation, unless the participants deliberately agree to change the purpose of the interaction.

Important considerations for design of activities:

— Why is this the best activity for the purpose? (learning outcomes)

— What level of capability do the participants have as they enter the activity?

— What new or elevated capabilities are to be developed during the activity, and how?

— How will you optimise socialisation and collaboration to enable sharing of diverse perspectives?

— How will you monitor learning during the experience?

— How will the group capture the outputs and in what format?

— Is the activity physically and psychologically safe for this group of people?

— What questions do you ask before, during, and after to remain aligned with the purpose?

— What happens after this activity to ensure the value is achieved beyond the activity?

6. How to facilitate interactions with positive impact

Recommended generic steps to design an effective interaction (or series of workshops) are:

1. Assess the foundational capabilities (knowledge, or Knowing; skills, or Doing; and social/cultural, or Being) of participants to determine current state and desired outcomes.

2. Consider the context of the interaction and the challenges to be resolved within this.

3. Define desired outcomes in terms of capabilities (Knowing, Doing and Being).

4. Create a series of activities that are inclusive social experiences in which participants explore possibilities relevant to the purpose and context.

5. Consider how to safely provoke divergent thinking and social exchanges around possibilities.

6. Discuss outputs and outcomes in reflective conversations to reinforce value generated.

7. Engage participants to provide meaningful feedback. Feedback is optimal when it highlights the aspects that have been done well (demonstrated capabilities against planned learning outcomes) and the aspects that they could have done better (expected aspects not met).

8. Facilitate a reflective conversation to summarise outcomes and next steps.

9. Extend the learning into professional practice. Assessing the impacts generated when capabilities are put into professional practice is helpful to refine capabilities.

BECOMING ADAPTABLE

Ongoing support beyond the planned learning activity helps to reinforce, amplify and extend value creation for the learning activity. Follow-up conversations after the activity enable the participants to consciously reflect on their progress. Assessing the impact of implementation is helpful for refining capabilities.

Facilitation insights

One of the key reasons to facilitate conversations is to engage participants in a social experience from which they learn, take more informed actions, or influence others. Pure facilitation is a neutral role, in which the facilitator does not bring a perspective to the argument but engages the participants in a way that draws out the full diversity of views for constructive discussion. In contrast, traditional teaching is a one-way transfer of existing knowledge from the teacher to the students. The facilitation approach advocated in this book is the opposite of the traditional approach. The Reverse Bloom Learning Framework (RBLF) is recommended to achieve the best results (Shelley 2020b).

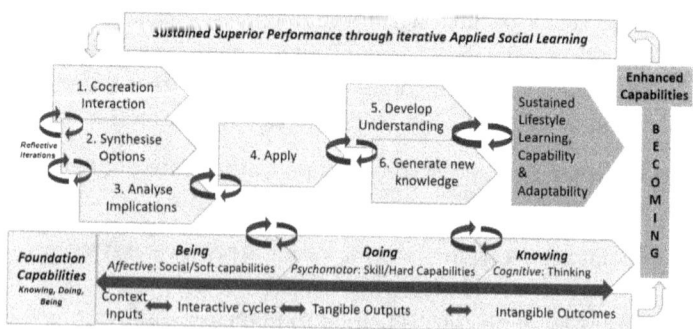

Figure 6.1. Reverse Bloom Learning Framework (RBLF)

6. How to facilitate interactions with positive impact

Figure 6.1 shows the overall structure of Reverse Bloom Learning Framework. Put simply, this involves reversing the traditional learning approach. The traditional method of teaching starts with remembering shared knowledge, then proceeding through deeper levels of ability on the topic, to understanding, application, analysis, synthesis, and finally the ability to create new insights.

RBLF goes in the opposite direction, starting with cocreation of insights (through inclusive conversations), which enables the synthesis of options to be analysed and prioritised for action. Application of the ideas generated through this process enables synthesis of insights and this generates new knowledge. The RBLF is effectively a social process that engages participants in knowledge cocreation. Its inputs from the facilitator are questions and from the participants their experiences, prior knowledge, and life experiences. This rich blend of insights, when facilitated collaboratively and safely, accelerates the learning of everyone involved and moves the collective knowledge to a higher level.

A workshop activity may be a complete cycle through the entire RBLF, or just a subset of the six steps shown in Figure 6.1, depending on the desired outcomes. A flow of activities though an entire RBLF cycle (steps 1-6) will generate the best outcomes, especially when effort is invested to include experiences across the three aspects of capability (*Knowing, Doing* and *Being*)

The process through the six steps is not as clear-cut as is indicated in Figure 6.1. Typically, participants will bounce forward and back though iterative loops in a more agile approach. In optimal facilitated activities, all three aspects of capability development (*Knowing, Doing* and *Being*) will be designed into the experience for the participants.

Being is about the relationships, cultural, and behavioural aspects of the experience. Although the social engagement of the interaction happens throughout all stages, it is most critical to address in the early stages (steps 1-3). Steps 1-3 are run in parallel with

BECOMING ADAPTABLE

each other as iterative cycles of divergent and convergent conversations. The outcome of these three steps is a plan of action or a prototype to test in practice.

When setting the context and atmosphere for an activity (before the actual activities start), it is important to establish expectations that encourage participants to be open and understand that they are engaging in a collaborative experience in a social learning environment. It helps if they understand that the experience is likely to be a bit different from their past experiences, so that they remain confident in the uncertainty of exploring unfamiliar themes. The more people are open to sharing with each other, the better the outcomes. The more they explore differences in perspectives and converse to understand the foundations of these differences, the more value will be cocreated.

There is a fine art to creating a safe social atmosphere, balancing familiarity with a novel context, to stimulate a creative flow and connect people so that they willingly collaborate. People will not share if they are stretched too far outside their comfort zones. Conversely, if they remain completely within their comfort zones, they are less likely to generate new thinking and less inclined to be open to ideas that do not fit their current perspectives. The ideal ecosystem is where participants are aware they will be at the edge of their comfort zone. They need to be confident that if they share some alternative thinking it will be respected and explored rather than rejected. Bringing this social ecosystem into reality is the biggest challenge for the facilitator. Once it is achieved, the cocreative magic starts to flow.

Doing focuses on applying the output from steps 1-3. This primarily happens in step 4, with occasional glances back into step 3, to assess progress, and forward into step 5, to ensure participants understand what is happening and why. Application (step 4) tests whether the plan or prototype performed to expectations and why (or why not).

6. How to facilitate interactions with positive impact

Applying what has been shared is an element often missed in formal education. Is it one thing to know and understand something, but another level completely to apply it well to generate a result in practice. Knowing the rules of a sport may be a component of success; it is the skilful application of this knowledge in practice that makes a champion.

Experimenting with the application of their ideas from steps 1-3, to see whether they work as expected, is critical to developing participants' capabilities. This is also true of facilitation capabilities. A skilled facilitator can make it look so simple to read the room, engage people to collaborate, and motivate them to cocreate new options. When a less seasoned facilitator tries to replicate those actions like a formula, they soon discover it is not as simple as it appeared to be. Every interaction is different and the flow in each version is different because of subtle, complex shifts between people and the ecosystem.

Knowing is about the generation and transfer of knowledge, which includes knowledge acquisition, theoretical elements, and cognitive aspects of learning. This happens primarily in the later stages of the cycle (steps 5-6) as the learning points start to take a more solid meaning. It is reinforced through reflective conversations justifying the new insights and challenging each other on what this means. Like *Being* and *Doing*, the *Knowing* aspect develops throughout all six steps. For example, the social exchange of insights and experiences in steps 1-3 increases the knowledge of all participants; and step 4 (*apply*) also increases knowledge through observation.

In summary, the facilitator is a catalyst, not an ingredient in the Reverse Bloom Learning Framework. They accelerate the interactions between the participants without influencing the content of the exchanges. They are more effective when asking provocative questions of the participants, drawing in the collective insights and stories from the room, than when sharing their own perspectives.

BECOMING ADAPTABLE

When the majority of the exchange of ideas comes from the participants themselves, they own the dialogue and the outputs and outcomes it generates. That sense of ownership makes the learning more likely to be applied later than content shared from a traditional trainer. Don't underestimate the importance of physical and psychological safety to build a trusted ecosystem and generate the best outcomes.

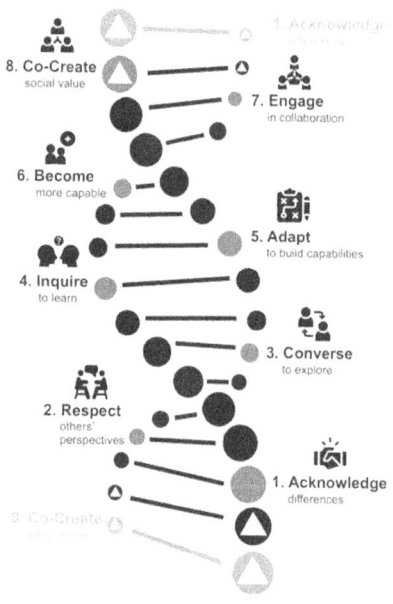

Figure 6.2. Collaborative Conversations Spiral

The Collaborative Conversations Spiral (Figure 6.2) shows how participants can amplify the social aspects of being into their interactions. The spiral represents a series of eight steps that occur in successful conversations as the interactions twist their way towards

7. Examples of facilitation activities

a higher level of understanding and maturity. The eight steps do not happen in isolation. Each new conversation feeds off an earlier conversation and this in turn leads into another.

Collaborative conversations are a spiral, rather than a cycle: each iteration takes the participants from an initial foundation to a higher level of knowledge and relationships than before (whereas a cycle brings participants back to the same starting point). Each iteration of the spiral's eight steps elevates us to a new shared perspective, which informs where we seek to go next. In the very best conversation spirals, the direction emerges as we go through each iteration and we end up in places we could not have imagined without going through the conversations together. The socialisation of many perspectives enables the mixing of ideas to cocreate new possibilities that any one party would not have generated alone.

Collaborative conversations are represented in Figure 6.2 as a double helix structure for two reasons. Firstly, such conversations involve two or more perspectives intertwined with each other through the steps, each influencing the other like strands of DNA in our genes. Second, success is accelerated though embedding these eight steps into our behavioural DNA, to become the natural and intuitive way we interact. Whilst at first we may need to consciously consider the steps to ensure we do them all in order, we soon learn the process and it seems very natural. It is like learning to dance: you start by counting the steps ("one, two, backstep…") in your head as you go, and as you practise the flow of the music becomes associated in your subconscious with a sequence of movements. Soon you are just enjoying your partner's smile as you smoothly swerve through the steps without thinking about the process itself.

As you finish one conversation spiral, it becomes obvious what you should address next in the next interaction and the conversations flow though the upward spiral. If your conversations are in a negative spiral towards conflict, you are probably skipping or ignoring steps and this is agitating your conversation partners.

BECOMING ADAPTABLE

Typically, this happens when the 'acknowledge differences' and 'inquire to learn' steps are overridden by a participant advocating their own ideas to push an agenda (and effectively disrespecting others).

When shared or facilitated in this way, collaborative conversations accelerate outcomes with each iteration to achieve more than earlier iterations.

A preliminary conversation to walk participants through the process can establish the appropriate atmosphere before the planned activity begins. Demonstrating and role-modelling each step provides clarity and builds confidence among the participants. This increases engagement and elevates the social aspects of the interactions. The result is richer exchanges that leverage the perspectives of all participants in a more effective way.

Guiding principles for OrgZoo facilitation

People have often asked what the rules are for facilitating OrgZoo activities. However, rules are not the optimal way to achieve success as they assume control and are too rigid. Rules can apply where a situation is absolute, inanimate and static. In contrast, life, relationships, personal and professional development, and culture are not absolutes. They are complex, subjective and unpredictable, making it inappropriate to attempt to bind them into a set of rules.

Social interactions are deeply influenced by the diversity of those involved, and their perceptions. Opening up conversations to constructively explore difference brings creative learning and builds relationships and trust. Closing out or criticising others, often because of ill-informed subconscious bias, destroys trust and relationships. An effective facilitator needs to be critically aware of the dynamics in the room. It is the facilitator's role to engage participants in sharing and to ensure their psychological safety.

7. Examples of facilitation activities

The guiding principles remind us of the wider contexts in which people interact and how changeable this is. These principles can apply to any facilitation around social learning and are the foundation of safe OrgZoo facilitation.

1. Behavioural adaptability is fundamental for sustained success.

2. Proactive, conscious choice of behaviour is better than subconscious reaction.

3. Inclusive *Conversations That Matter* are critical for mutual understanding.

4. Culture is defined by the more influential animals in your Zoo and their relationships.

5. All OrgZoo characters can be found in most social contexts; some may be elusive.

6. Every OrgZoo character has a place in the ecosystem, but they can become misaligned with context and desired outcomes.

7. Behaviours are not absolute (right or wrong): they can be perceived differently.

8. Culture is a subjective interpretation that usually has exceptions.

9. Behavioural DNA can be reliably visualised through inclusive cocreation activities.

10. Diversity of behaviour can be (if facilitated well) a source of learning rather than conflict.

11. Unfamiliar behaviours can be learned and refined through role-play and gamified activities.

12. "Which character am I?" is a misinformed question — rather, ask "Which is best to be here and now?"

BECOMING ADAPTABLE

The principles cover many of the contexts in which you can use the OrgZoo creative metaphor to design activities that help people to expand their behavioural comfort zones, and therefore achieve better relationship outcomes. The list of principles is not comprehensive: I am sure you can suggest useful additions.

Elevating participation

As highlighted earlier, the best conversations are social, experiential and developmental, and lead to mutually agreed actions and value creation. That is, the best conversations are an open exchange of perspectives through which all participants become more informed. This generates enhanced relationships and leads to creation of social value. Such outcomes are not achieved by accident; they arise from careful planning and a deep understanding of the values, cultural norms, behaviours and expectations of the stakeholders with whom you are engaging.

This is all good in theory, but what does it mean in practice? Much of the value in the interactions comes from the exchange between the participants. The facilitator creates the environment in which people feel confident to share insights and half-formed ideas. This can at first feel uncomfortable for the participants, because they are used to more formal environments and only offering ideas that they are quite sure of.

Building trust between the participants will enable them to venture outside their comfort zone. When they do this, they share half-baked ideas that are still quite malleable. In this form the ideas are more easily combined to create hybrid ideas; and the social exchanges between the participants accelerates this. As a facilitator I find it is best to be open about my intention to stretch people beyond their comfort zone and about the reasons for doing this. Once participants understand what is happening, they are more inclined to join in the

7. Examples of facilitation activities

process. They soon become familiar with this feeling and adapt as others around them also practice the social exchanges. A group working together soon develops a higher degree of comfort, knowing that this stretching will accelerate their own development and the collaboration efforts of the whole group.

There are some key characteristics of applied social learning systems that enable the best outcomes from such activities (Shelley and Goodwin 2018). These include encouraging and modelling:

— openness
— curiosity
— creativity, including a mindset of social cocreation
— emergence (exploratory)
— experiential
— divergence
— courage
— confidence, despite being outside comfort zone
— and, most importantly, enjoyable: the best learning is fun

Emphasise social interactions early in the activities to create awareness of the benefits of social connection and flow. Highlight in your introductions that workshops generate the best outcomes when facilitated as iterative action learning cycles. As participants constructively engage and build trust, confidence emerges.

The list of principles below is not meant to be comprehensive, but offers a useful foundation for designing and facilitating interactions (Shelley 2020b).

— Engage to open minds rather than fill them, emphasise context over content.
— Aim to cocreate a range of options rather than finding an existing answer.

BECOMING ADAPTABLE

- Embed iterative collaborative cycles of divergent and convergent thinking, laced with social challenges to explore the emotional and human aspects of the topics.
- Reinforce that creativity is a critical part of learning, as are sensemaking and play.
- Stimulate Creative Friction (constructive challenges to deliberately clash alternatives to cocreate new possibilities) as a key driver.
- Proactively facilitate learner-centred experiences, with balanced cognitive, affective and psychomotor aspects.
- Optimal learning builds the capabilities and confidence of the learner to safely enter the unknown and explore (expanding their comfort zone).
- Social connections and trusted relationships should be outcomes of the learning
- Invest heavily in reflective conversations through collaborative cycles to share perspectives.
- Invest in designs and facilitation that are inclusive of all perspectives.
- Aim to develop well-rounded people who feel competent to generate value from applying collaborative learning to continue to refine their capabilities ongoing.

Active engagement of participants aligned with these principles will amplify the value created and the intangible outcomes, such as trust, relationships and enjoyment. This ultimately increases adaptability and capabilities.

7. Examples of facilitation activities

This chapter describes a range of OrgZoo activities that enable participants to start *Becoming Adaptable*, and explanations on how to apply these techniques well.

Whilst the design features and nuances of activities may be obvious to an experienced OrgZoo practitioner, they will not necessarily be clear for people unfamiliar with OrgZoo approach and philosophy. There are dangers in doing these activities with little knowledge and following the steps like a recipe. Treating them as basic games for fun, rather than strategic learning activities, is likely to lead to sub-optimal outcomes at best, and at worst to confusion or conflict. Although the activities are fun, the fun element is what makes it engaging for participants, not the focus of the activity. The fun element is beneficial as it helps to engage participants in deep personal or professional development whilst enjoying the experience.

Please do not use these approaches to categorise a person into a specific type. This is the exact opposite of what OrgZoo was

BECOMING ADAPTABLE

designed to achieve. Categorising a person as one OrgZoo character is not helpful, unless you are describing a specific behaviour in a specific moment and situation. In many situations, an adaptable person can be playing a couple of behaviours in parallel for best effect.

These activities should open minds to explore how many possible characters (behaviours) a person can adopt. They should assist people to make choices about which characters are most appropriate in a context. This helps them to choose how to change behaviours as the situation emerges, and ultimately to build their confidence as a role model to drive change in a specific direction.

There are many ways OrgZoo can be used for facilitation to develop behavioural awareness and adaptability. The most common ways to create inclusive, social, safe and enjoyable interactions are described below. For more ways to apply OrgZoo, join OZAN (see chapter 9) and share insights with experienced mentors.

The techniques described below are simplified and generalised to assist new facilitators with learning the basics. Advanced practitioners typically adapt these techniques, based on their experiences, to achieve specific desired outcomes with different groups of participants. Sometimes this is as simple as adjusting the question asked or the ways the participants are grouped to explore different aspects of the question. Other times the facilitator will connect the OrgZoo approach with another tool.

As discussed in the design section of this chapter, the structure of an OrgZoo activity is based on the five key elements of *Conversations That Matter*:

1. Purpose: what am I trying to achieve?
2. Outputs: tangible artefacts and results generated
3. Outcomes: intangible impacts generated

7. Examples of facilitation activities

4. Benefits: value created by the interactions, outputs and outcomes

5. Beneficiaries: who receives these benefits?

It is important that the facilitator thinks about these elements before doing the activity. Ideally write them down or say them aloud to challenge what you think you plan to do. I routinely put this information into a one-page brief for a client, as part of the planning discussion and agreement. This ensures we are covering their expectations. Articulating the five elements can lead to insights about how the approach will fare with the participants and other stakeholders.

The activity descriptions in this section include process steps, insights and useful provocative questions for facilitators. These are the tips I would normally share when mentoring inexperienced facilitators, to mitigate risks and optimise outcomes. This additional guidance is based on learnings from practitioners who have done the activity before.

Even with all this preparation, there can still be disruptive participants to engage with and accommodate as smoothly as possible. Sometimes this disruption can be because their level of capability is too far below the required foundations for your activity (see Reverse Bloom Learning Framework in Chapter 6), in which case you may have to separate people into similar levels of competency or help them individually. Alternatively, it is possible that one or more members have an alternative or hidden agenda for the activity, in which case you need to manage the situation carefully. Normally a reference to the agreed purpose or referring the challenge to the 'parking lot' for follow-up later is sufficient. However, Rattlesnake, Lion and Vulture behaviours can sometimes require stronger leadership, and all the adaptability you have, to maintain a sense of achievement and to minimise the disruption of a determined resistance.

BECOMING ADAPTABLE

In OrgZoo interactions people often ask a misinformed question like "Which animal am I?" This is misinformed because it implies behaviour is fixed; but the goal is to behave as the most appropriate character in the situation you are in (or plan to be in). When such questions are asked, support the participant and engage in constructive conversation around the question, including others if this can be done without making the participant feel small or incompetent. This is when the facilitator needs to be a role model, constructively and respectfully addressing questions and leading by example with their professionalism. Often if one person is not sure of what needs to happen, others are also unsure but not confident enough to ask. Reward the one who is courageous enough to ask, and build the confidence of others by making it a positive experience for all participants. It is the facilitator's role to ensure that all participants are appropriately informed and feeling safe.

The ability to be a role model who elevates the spirit and culture of a situation is a strength that great leaders seem to be naturals at. For most, though, this talent does not happen without practice. We can all become more adaptable through practising a range of characters in the activities below. One fun way to do this is Behavioural Improvisation. Another way is to plan for a range of possibilities and match your behavioural choice to those possibilities in advance. All of these 'learning games' enable you, and those learning with you in the social experience, to develop confidence in making behavioural choices. This ability to pre-think the possible outcomes and choose behaviours to adopt whilst in the situation generates better results more often. Being prepared stimulates confidence, which in itself elevates chances of success. However, it is always possible that something you did not predict happens. Then it is even more important to be able to adapt on the fly to achieve best outcomes.

An adaptable person can quickly switch to any of the characters in response to a shift in the situation. A master at adaptation can

7. Examples of facilitation activities

change the environment by choosing behaviours that lead others to change with them, shifting the whole group to a better situation. Mastering your adaptability requires practice and is accelerated by feedback from trusted friends on how you are developing.

One significant step towards achieving mastery is the ability to match the character (behaviour) with the current (or desired) situation. This comes by engaging in conversations with others about which characters are best in which situations and reflecting on why. There will be differences of opinion, and seemingly opposite opinions can both be correct. Behaviour and social interactions are subjective states that are perceived in different ways by different people. Understanding the diversity of these possible perceptions can provide deep insights and accelerate your development. Always ask questions about why. This is not disrespectful. In fact, if you are prepared to engage in a Collaborative Conversation (as described earlier in this chapter) about differences, it is deeply respectful as you are demonstrating your interest in understanding their perspective.

Activity 7.1 OrgZoo Character Introductions

This activity is a quick ice-breaker to engage people in conversation, whilst learning a little about each other and the OrgZoo characters.

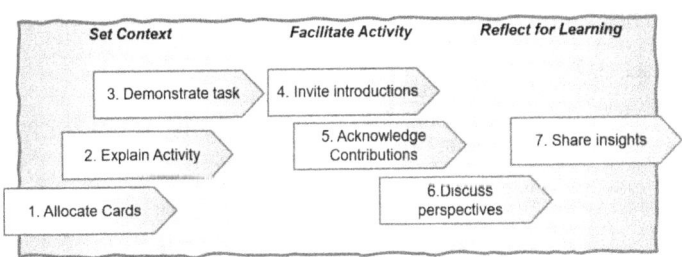

Figure 7.1.1. Overview of activity: OrgZoo Character Introductions

BECOMING ADAPTABLE

Purpose

A quick and fun way to get people relaxed about sharing their thoughts with others in the room. Introductions are important where people do not know each other, as there will not be any trust where there are no relationships. Traditional introductions can be a bit dry and can often go too long, as some people overshare. OrgZoo character introductions stimulate short useful exchanges and are an engaging ice breaker.

Outputs

No specific output other than some people taking notes about who is in the room.

Outcomes

People feel more comfortable knowing who is in the room with them and this will encourage them to share and participate more in subsequent activities. This way of introducing ourselves stimulates the creative process, which is beneficial for collaborative activities.

Benefits

Increased confidence to participate, starting of open conversations, a sense of inclusiveness and connection.

Beneficiaries

All participants benefit from being involved in open conversations in which everyone participates.

The facilitator benefits as they get some sense of the people in the room, making facilitation of subsequent activities smoother.

Indirectly, peers of the participants benefit as the person will

7. Examples of facilitation activities

return to their normal places of interaction being more adaptable having experienced the value of constructive development activities.

Process

1: Allocate cards. Randomly allocate one OrgZoo card to each participant. Make it clear they are randomly distributed (to prevent people worrying about being classified).

2: Explain activity. Ask each participant to introduce themselves (name only) within the context of this character.

Suggest they share when they are like this character and when they are NOT like this character.

Highlight that this is just a quick fun ice breaker to get people talking and share.

State that you only want each person to talk for no longer than a minute for this activity.

3: Demonstrate task. Consider introducing yourself using the process to get the activity started (builds confidence) and demonstrate how to do it briefly (see insights below).

4: Invite introductions. Ask if any participant wishes to go first (stimulating a sense of autonomy).

5: Acknowledge contributions. Thank each participant for their contribution as you move through all participants, ensuring to manage time and not allow the ice breaker to eat into the time allocated for other planned activities. If you have plenty of time and need to invest in developing trust and relationships, plan more time for this activity.

6: Discuss perspectives. Thank people for their participation, highlighting that participation is important throughout all the planned activities. Reinforce that there are

BECOMING ADAPTABLE

many perceptions of behaviour and that their interactions with each other will be more productive if people are aware of and respect this. This is a good moment to quickly walk through *Collaborative Conversations* if you have not already do so, to set the scene for optimal collaboration.

7: Share insights. Ask if anyone would like to share any insights before you move on. After this activity it is usual for people to be quite relaxed about engaging and sharing in group discussions and they are a little familiar with the OrgZoo characters. This is helpful for the more advanced activities they will encounter in later experiences.

Insights

It can be helpful to encourage people to just listen to others, rather than take notes during this activity. Sometimes people can be nervous about sharing personal insights if others are recording (audio or written). Open sharing and trust are generated by just socialising with each other, especially if this is a first activity in which participants are engaging.

If people know each other quite well and there is a positive culture, a more advanced way to play this activity is to organise people in pairs and get a partner to introduce the other (still in reference to the randomly allocated character). The risk to avoid with this is someone sharing an inappropriate story about the partner. It is best to get the partners to agree what can be shared in the introduction — and what should not be shared — to avoid any danger of this happening.

I find it helpful to be a role model and share my own example before asking others to do that. Stick strictly to the process and keep it short to demonstrate that you just want an ice-breaker.

7. Examples of facilitation activities

For example:

> "Hi, my name is Arthur and I have drawn the character of Owl, the eternal mentor. I absolutely identify with this character as I am feeling at my best when I am helping others. As the facilitator of this activity, there are times when I need to shift into Lion mode to control the time and keep things moving."

Or:

> "Hi, my name is Arthur and I have difficulty identifying with this Vulture character. I am normally a very positive person and willing to share information to help others, but the Vulture seems overly critical to me. I guess I use this critical behaviour when I see problems and call them out, to try to rectify them before they become a major challenge."

Be aware of how many people you have in the room, as it takes at least a minute for each person to answer this activity. There are inevitably some people who desire to share their life story when given the floor, and this is where you need to step up and manage the time closely. If you allow one person to speak for a long time and not others, you will disengage the group. Make a bit of fun with this by 'playing' the characters to manage the situation: "Thanks Fred, I need to switch to Lion now to keep the show moving. Susan, you're next..."

The key questions to ask for this activity are:

— When am I like this character? The answer may be, "I just do not identify with this behaviour myself."

— When I am not like this character? Exploring this question highlights that there are contexts in which that behaviour can be useful.

BECOMING ADAPTABLE

Activity 7.2 Behavioural DNA

Behavioural DNA is the most powerful and strategic activity in the OrgZoo repertoire. It enables the people in the conversation to quickly generate a visual representation of the behavioural profile of any situation they wish to explore. Participants cocreate a heatmap image by sorting the OrgZoo character cards into four categories for a given situation. Figure 7.2.1 provides an overview of the steps in the activity.

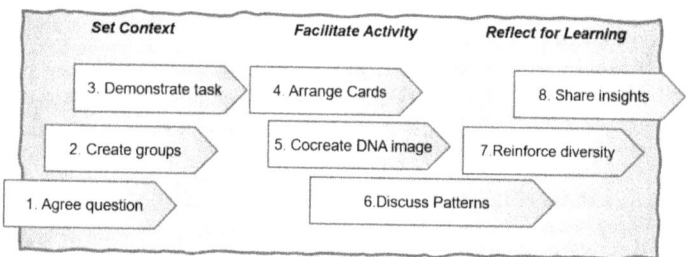

Figure 7.2.1. Overview of steps in Behavioural DNA activity

For example, the facilitator asks what is the behavioural profile of a specific context. This could be collaborative leadership, our team in crisis, creativity... literally any situation of interest. Usually the workshop participants are broken into smaller groups of 2-5 people (three is ideal). This generates a conversation in small groups to deeply involve everyone in an exchange of views of where each behaviour fits from their perspective.

Each group adds their agreed profile to the overall image, creating a pattern that collectively represents the opinions of the whole group. This combined image highlights similarities and differences in that group and usually engages the whole group in a higher-level conversation. The facilitator encourages discussions about the differences in perspectives, using the visual as a conversation stimulant to highlight examples in the composite Behavioural DNA image.

7. Examples of facilitation activities

Figure 7.2.2. Example group arrangement of the character cards for Behavioural DNA

Figure 7.2.3 shows the composite Behavioural DNA from six groups. Numbered columns represent the groups and a coloured cell in the columns below this indicates this group's selected characters in that category. For example, in this activity group 1 selected Bee, Insect (beneficial), Mouse, Owl and Quercus in the 'expected' category.

The degree of similarity or difference in the placement of the characters into each of the four layers provides insights into the degree of diversity there is among the participants. The Behavioural DNA represents their collective perspectives on the culture (team, organisation or stereotypical/perceived culture).

Post creation, the Behavioural DNA output can stimulate rich conversations about the appropriateness of the behavioural characteristics of the target group. It is often useful to share a Behavioural

BECOMING ADAPTABLE

DNA image from a different group to extend the conversation, once the group has discussed their own thoughts on their image. This can provide excellent cultural insights that may not be obvious without this third conversation (after small group and large group comparisons).

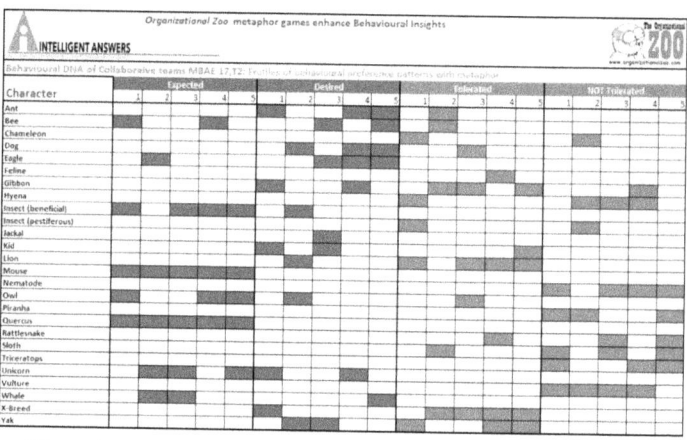

Figure 7.2.3. Example Behavioural DNA image from an activity involving five groups

Behavioural DNA has been used as a visualisation of the culture in past, present and future contexts, to enable participants to literally see what their culture is perceived to be. This leads them to engage in constructive dialogue about implications and appropriateness to guide cultural change (or stabilise desirable elements) and highlight what is best to change and why.

Purpose

The purpose of this activity varies depending on the group and the question being explored. Typically this will be a combination of:

— stimulating rich conversations about behavioural

7. Examples of facilitation activities

profiles and culture as assessed by the people in the conversations.

— cocreating a visual image of a culture and where the similarities and differences are.

— stimulating dialogue around the origins of the differences in perspectives of a culture, and constructively discussing these to develop deeper relationships and understanding of each other.

— being a foundation of cultural changes from which shifts in behaviour can be measured over time.

— enabling the comparison of expected, desired, tolerated, and rejected behaviours in different cultures.

Outputs

An arrangement of character cards for each group that represents their collective opinions.

Behavioural DNA image created from collated group results.

Images of the activity, often shared in social media and for recording the activity.

Outcomes

The outcomes of the activity vary enormously depending on the people in the conversation, the questions asked, and the purpose they were addressing. The outcomes are more important than the outputs, as this is where the learning and relationships are built.

Below is a generic list of example outcomes that can be achieved when this activity is well facilitated. Although it is not comprehensive, it provides a good understanding of the range of possible outcomes.

BECOMING ADAPTABLE

- People enlightened by Collaborative Conversations about behaviour.
- Strengthened understanding of each other among participants in the workshop.
- Deeper understanding of chosen topic to explore: leadership, creativity, collaboration, culture, who we are, who we would like to be, understanding of our stakeholders, behavioural strengths and weaknesses of our competitors and ourselves, how we can adapt our behavioural capabilities… anything involving people interacting with each other or even self-development.
- Enhanced capabilities to engage in inclusive conversations around differences of perspectives.
- Stronger relationships and trust.
- Increased confidence to cocreate new insights and knowledge.
- Appreciation of the power of gamified learning in social contexts.
- Enjoyment of learning in a safe, socialised and inclusive experience.
- Deeper understanding of the power of Organizational Zoo character cards (and virtual equivalent).

Benefits

Increased cultural awareness as a foundation to cultural change.

Build a set of behavioural profiles over time to monitor change.

Provide easily understood artefacts to stimulate engagement.

7. Examples of facilitation activities

Ability to assess the full diversity of views and understand the appropriateness of behavioural choices.

Beneficiaries

Everyone in the conversation.

People who were not in the conversation, who can access the outputs to learn for the insights.

Stakeholders of the participants who are engaged more productively in future.

Process

Typically steps 1-4 take around 15 minutes. Reflective discussion on the Behavioural DNA can take as long as you desire, or as much time as you have available, to explore the diversity of views (see insights below for some examples). Although it can be done quickly, a good group can engage in stimulating conversations of more than an hour when the questions asked are of high quality and the group has quite diverse views. The more diverse the group (culture, gender, age, professions etc), the greater the diversity of results and the richer the conversation.

It can be useful to show a Behavioural DNA image to give participants an indication of what the output looks like. If doing this, try to select one that either aligns with the topic you have chosen or contrasts with it (depending on what you want to stimulate).

Inputs required:

— Groups of people prepared to engage in Collaborative Conversations.

— OrgZoo character cards or virtual equivalent: one set per group.

BECOMING ADAPTABLE

— Behavioural DNA macro (spreadsheet to generate the Behavioural DNA image).

1: Agree question. Set the context to be discussed, or ask what topic the participants wish to explore. Write it in a place that everyone can see, to maintain consistency.

Be as specific as possible and ensure the topic is relevant to the learning outcomes. For example, the behavioural profile of 'leadership' may not be specific enough. You may benefit from breaking it down to leadership in a crisis, or leadership when everything is running smoothly. Perhaps half your groups do one situation and the other half do the other context to provide a comparative Behavioural DNA. This enables comparison of diversity within a situation and how this differs from another context; for example, the team when brainstorming or when about to pitch the proposal to the decision makers. For self-reflection, this could be me when I am mentoring versus me when I am in problem-solving mode. Appropriateness of behaviour is very contextual. If you ask a generic question, you will get a stereotypical profile which averages out the collective behaviours. A stereotypical answer is rarely a good choice in a specific instance.

Another good way to do comparative Behavioural DNA is to compare the profile of a person or team over time — past, present, and desired future. For example, our current culture versus our desired future culture.

There are many other ways to use this tool — for more ideas see the insights at the end of this section.

2: Create groups. Break the participants into groups of 2-5 people (three is ideal) and provide each with one set of

7. Examples of facilitation activities

OrgZoo cards (one of each of the characters, A-Y).

Provide two sets of character cards if you want each group to do a comparative Behavioural DNA (for example, current and future, our team and the competitor).

3: Demonstrate task. Ask the subgroups to sort the cards into four categories, depending on the nature of the challenge being discussed. Remind them to discuss placement or movement of each character and that there are no right or wrong answers — just their perspectives.

If self-reflecting, the four categories will be: mostly; usually; not usually; and rarely. For example:

— When I am at my best/worst /stressed/in conflict I am... (place cards in each category)

— When we are at our best/worst /stressed/in conflict we typically are ...

If a group is discussing the behavioural profile of a team or organisation in a known context, the same four categories can be used. Sometimes it may more appropriate to change the words to expected (must haves), desired (also useful to have), tolerated (prefer not to have), and rejected (if this behaviour is observed, we will speak to the person and ask they stop doing this).

For example, if a team is looking at a future desired culture to be achieved, we ask:

When we become the culture we wish to be, which characters would we expect to see, which would we also desire to have, which ones would we reluctantly allow to happen, and which would we immediately speak to the person and ask to desist... (place cards in each category).

BECOMING ADAPTABLE

This wording is also useful for assessing a more distant culture, for example the characteristics of a competitor. What would we expect them to be, what do we think they also desire, what do we think they would tolerate and what would they reject?

4: Arrange cards. Ask each group to sort the cards into the four categories. Encourage them to be in open conversation during this activity and to explain why they have put cards in the categories. Encourage them to share different perspectives.

If there is a lot of argument about any particular card, put it aside.

It should take around 15 minutes for groups to sort their cards. If some groups are stuck, assist them by asking questions and clarifying. It can take longer when the groups are multicultural and when people are not interacting in their native language.

Encourage groups to go with their initial feelings about the characters, trying not to over-analyse.

Once a group is comfortable with their arrangement of characters into the categories, ask them to walk around the room and, without interfering, observe what others have done. During this time take a photo of each group's output (the card arrangement) and enter the characters into the Behavioural DNA spreadsheet.

It is a good idea to plan this activity to occur just before a break, as this provides slower groups more time to finish and allows more time for the facilitator to construct the Behavioural DNA image. Typically, it takes about one minute to enter each group's data and another couple of minutes to create and format the image ready for display.

7. Examples of facilitation activities

During the break participants can engage with others about their outputs and the process.

5: Cocreate Behavioural DNA image. The Behavioural DNA image can be manually drawn, but this is very time consuming. The most efficient method is to take a photo of each group's output and use this to enter the selections into the Behavioural DNA spreadsheet. The first letter of each character is added to the appropriate category in the file. An embedded macro generates the Behavioural DNA image when selections for all groups are entered.

The file containing the macro is available for download from the OZAN resources wiki (organizationalzoo.com).

Display the Behavioural DNA image and reflect on process. Highlight that this is a cocreated image that represents the inputs of everyone in the room. Ask if any participant wishes to share any insights from how they collaborated in group to achieve this outcome.

6: Discuss patterns. Facilitate a conversation about patterns, similarities and differences in the Behavioural DNA image.

This discussion is best as a facilitated discussion, rather than the facilitator interpreting the image.

Ask questions like:

— What jumps out at you from this image?

— What have we mostly agreed on? (clusters of colours together)

— Why do you think this is the case?

— What have we disagreed on? (examples where the characters are spread across diffcrent categories, especially across upper two as well as lower two).

BECOMING ADAPTABLE

— Why do you think this is the case?

— Who would like to ask another group about a specific placement of a character?

— What do you think this tells us about the overall profile?

Other relevant questions will arise depending on context and the target of the profile.

7: Reinforce diversity. Ask groups that selected seemingly opposite categories to share why they have put the character in the category they did. For example, if one group selected lion in 'expected' and another selected it in 'rejected' ask each group to share why. Facilitate a discussion about the reasons and whether they make sense to the other group and why or why not. This is a common occurrence in mixed cultural groups and is worth exploring to understand the range of expectations of different groups. There have been examples where a character has been selected in all four categories for the same question by different groups. This generated a rich dialogue when explored.

Reinforce that there are many perceptions of behaviour and that their interactions with each other will be more productive if participants respect this.

8: Share insights. Ask if anyone would like to share further insights before you move on.

Thank people for their participation, highlighting that participation is important throughout all the planned activities.

Insights

How you use this technique is almost endless. It is only limited by your imagination, while ensuring you remain

7. Examples of facilitation activities

within the psychological safety of the participants and ethical sensibilities. The activities can be quick starter exercises to familiarise the participants with the process and the characters to build confidence, or a much deeper and longer conversation about the cultural transformation an organisation needs to engage upon to optimise their performance. Both of these are real examples that were successful.

It is advisable to use some simple techniques as starters for a diverse group who are not familiar with the characters. This builds their confidence to share perceptions with others and be more influential in more complex conversations.

A quick quiz activity is a good way to kick this off, for example showing them the images of some of the characters and asking them what behaviours each character represents. Once they have shared their thoughts, bring up the characteristics from the OrgZoo book (Shelley 2007) and discuss the similarities and differences. When doing this, never say someone is wrong if they say something unexpected. Ask them why they see it that way and explore this with the others. The enhances the understanding of diversity of perception and helps build mutual understanding.

Supporting slides for all such starters are available from the OZAN resources database (organizationalzoo.com).

If you have time, ask groups who finish early to walk around and observe what other groups have done and the group dynamics. Make sure they do not interfere with the other conversations or participate in them. This observation provides them with some early insights about diversity of views and highlights to them that different groups are working through the process in different ways. These

BECOMING ADAPTABLE

observations can make the foundation of some rich conversations as additional learning, after the Behavioural DNA reflection. This way they remain engaged whilst they wait for the other groups to complete the activity.

Another way to extend the activity for early finishers is to ask them a challenging question. For example, if you have to remove one character for the pack completely, which would it be and why? Or, if they have many cards in one row and relatively few in another, ask them to discuss whether the rows could be more even (without forcing them to do so). A useful additional conversation is to ask them to discuss what they thought of the process they went through and report on this to the other groups at the end of the session. All of these interactions provide additional insights and ensure those completing the task quickly remain active and do not become distracted by other activities.

Activity 7.3 Behavioural Improvisation

Purpose

Behavioural Improvisation is a fun activity designed to increase awareness of the OrgZoo characters and to play the part of the characters on demand. Using this as a practice mechanism highlights where behaviours are aligned or misaligned in a conversation flow, or out of character.

Outputs

No specific output, unless the activity is video or audio recorded.

Outcomes

Elevated awareness of the characteristics of the characters (including others' perceptions).

7. Examples of facilitation activities

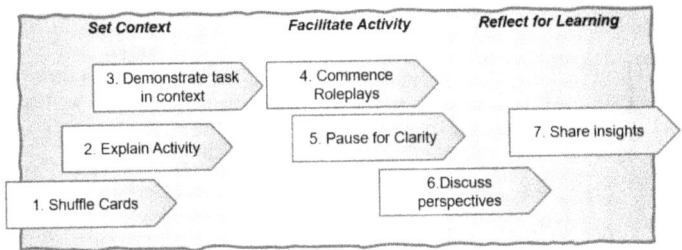

Figure 7.3 Overview of steps for Behavioural Improvisation activity

Increased confidence to act out the character behaviour in context of the conversation.

Enjoyment and connection between people playing the activity.

Benefits

Broader and deeper understanding of different behaviours.

Increased behavioural adaptability and greater capability to choose how to act.

Greater confidence to display a wider range of behaviours through impromptu practice.

Ability to manage one's own behaviours in uncertainty and make better behavioural choices.

Beneficiaries

Everyone in the activity.

People who were not in the activity who will benefit from interaction with a more adaptable person in future interactions.

BECOMING ADAPTABLE

Process

1: Shuffle cards. Shuffle two full sets of OrgZoo cards to ensure random distribution. Turn the double deck face-down on a table for each small group (3-5).

2: Explain activity. Describe the basic process as below.

Agree a situation for the conversation (to provide a context in which to participate).

The first participant turns over the top card and places it face-up on the table. They immediately start talking about the selected context, role-playing as the character on the new face-up card, and continue to do so for 15 seconds (use an audible timer).

When the timer sounds, the next participant (rotating clockwise) turns over the next card and continues the conversation, maintaining context but now role-playing the next character.

Repeat the process until all players have had at least two turns or the deck is fully expired.

Highlight the "Pause" (step 5) and explain.

3: Demonstrate the task in context. The facilitator demonstrates the role-play by selecting the top card and role-playing for 15 seconds, within the agreed context. Put the card back and reshuffle, ready for participants.

4: Commence role plays. Ask teams to start their timers and draw a new character card to role-play each time it rings.

The next person in the circle plays the next character drawn, connecting to what has happened previously as much as possible to continue the flow (despite the character change).

7. Examples of facilitation activities

Watch closely as some people may not be following the process. Assist them to correct it.

5: Pause for clarity. Any player can pause the activity for clarity by loudly stating "Stop the clock".

The purpose of this pause is to constructively challenge if the player is playing the character correctly within the context of the situation. The team can discuss this briefly and share their perspectives. This is not a correction but a sharing of differences to deepen insights.

6: Discuss perspectives. Upon completion of two cycles or the whole deck, open the conversation to discuss interpretations of the different characters. Players share enjoyable moments and discuss whether the roles as played would actually happen in that context. This helps them to reflect on the applicability of the behaviour and whether it is in alignment with the situation.

This is a good moment to reinforce Collaborative Conversations and discuss behavioural alignment in their organisation (or compare across organisations if the participants are from different places).

7: Share insights. Thank people for their participation and ask if anyone would like to share any insights about the experience before you move on.

Insights

This activity is a lot of fun and enjoyed by all who play it. It can also be a great ice-breaker for people who are already familiar with OrgZoo characters.

The adage 'practice makes perfect' is applicable to this activity. Getting participants to practise the behaviours on demand is a powerful way to increase their scope of behaviours and build their

BECOMING ADAPTABLE

confidence to choose them in real contexts. It is also a useful peer feedback mechanism to help people who may be misinterpreting which behaviours are appropriate to the context.

Activity 7.4 Behavioural Role-Plays

Purpose

OrgZoo Role-Plays are a way to write and act out scenarios to enable people to observe behavioural interactions in context. They are mini plays of a few minutes' duration to demonstrate a scenario from the perspective of one of the participants.

The idea is to act out a significant behavioural interaction or inflection point from their experience. This enables two benefits: firstly, they can share what they have experienced in a safe, anonymous, fun activity; and secondly, they receive feedback on others' perspectives of the appropriateness of the behaviours in that context.

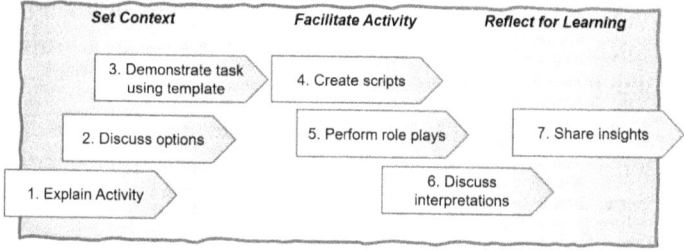

Figure 7.4.1. Overview of steps for Behavioural Role-Plays

Outputs

A scenario script (if written, drawn or in completed template).

No other specific output unless someone is taking notes or recording the role-play.

7. Examples of facilitation activities

Sometimes insights, feedback or lessons learnt, if these are being recorded.

Note: be aware that any outputs may be appropriately or inappropriately used or shared by others if they are recorded. See the 'insights' section below for more guidance on this point.

Outcomes

Elevated awareness of the interdependencies between behaviour and context.

Increased confidence to choose behaviour in context in future situations.

Enjoyment and connection between people creating and role-playing the activity.

Benefits

Broader and deeper understanding of different behavioural interaction in contexts.

Increased awareness of behavioural choices across scenarios.

Elevated confidence in their own adaptability and greater capability to choose how to act.

Greater confidence to provide feedback on behaviours for others.

Ability to manage one's own behaviours in uncertainty and make better behavioural choices.

Beneficiaries

Everyone involved in the role-plays.

People who were not in the conversation, who will interact more productively with participant.

BECOMING ADAPTABLE

Process

1: Explain activity. Discuss how role-plays help build familiarity with behavioural interactions and highlight the interdependencies between them (no behaviour happens isolation and how they each impact each other in the context). This will not be immediately evident to some participants.

Highlight that different people will sense the situation differently and that the feedback from others' perspectives is constructive insight to be aware of, not criticism.

The ideal scenario is a short exchange between two parties that highlights how their behaviour was aligned or misaligned and what the impact of this is. Typically, this is three or four interactions (of a sentence or two each) between the two parties. It is ideal if there is a shift in the behaviour stimulated by the behaviour of the other. This shift in behaviour highlights a key insight for the audience, which may vary depending on their own perspective.

2: Discuss options. The easiest way to create a script is to think about an actual scenario you have been exposed to and script it in the template using the OrgZoo character cards.

State that the whole role-play should only take about a minute and focus on the behavioural interactions.

It is OK to explain the context briefly, as long as the actual people in the real scenario remain anonymous and the emphasis is on learning, not attempting to embarrass anyone.

3: Demonstrate task using template. Before the activity, take a good example of a completed template that matches the context you are using, and use it to demonstrate the output.

7. Examples of facilitation activities

It is a good idea to read through the script or, better, act it out with a cofacilitator or participant. Then discuss the role-play in the group before asking the participants to create their own scripts. Remind the participants to genuinely play the script by acting it out with the body language and tone that you would expect as this is more engaging for all and develops richer interactions and reflections.

4: Create scripts. Arrange the participants to work on a script. Pairs are best, or small group sizes to match the number of people in the role-play, as then everyone gets to play a part.

Some teams will complete their scripts quite quickly. Ask them to go out of the room and practise their roles. Later groups may not get the time to practise. Fifteen minutes should be plenty to write a brief script if the participants are familiar with each other.

5: Perform role-plays. This is simply asking groups to perform their role-play and the audience members to write down what behaviours (OrgZoo characters) they observe in each player.

Using the OrgZoo characters as the common language to describe the observed behaviours helps to achieve a degree of consistency in the interpretations. This helps compare the perceptions between the observers; it may also contrast against what the players thought they were displaying. People are often unaware of how others perceive their behaviour and it can be very different from what they thought they were doing. One person's assertive can appear aggressive to another.

Note: Acting a role may make some people uncomfortable, but usually with a little encouragement most will participate.

BECOMING ADAPTABLE

Do not force anyone who does not wish to play a role to do so. They can be given a role as observer, commentator or insights recorder, or some other way of participating. Try to involve everyone as much as possible and make it a light-hearted fun experience.

6: Discuss interpretations. After each role play, ask some audience participants to share their interpretation of the behaviours being played and whether this is aligned with context. Constructively discuss if other behavioural choices may also have worked in the situation.

Ask about the timing of the inflection of one behaviour to another in the context of the story.

7: Share insights. Ask if there are any insights anyone would like to share before you move on.

Ask participants to highlight some moments of inspiration from the role-plays as feedback to the players. Reinforce any situations where there were differences in perceptions of behaviour the flow in the conversation to increase the learning.

Thank people for their participation, highlighting that social participation and awareness of others in context is important for building relationships and stimulating rich reflective discussions.

Observe how the short, simple scenario below highlights a behavioural change in both characters within the context of the situation.

Shorter with focus on the behavioural interactions is better than long scripts with other aspects that are not critical to understanding the behaviours and their impact on outcomes.

7. Examples of facilitation activities

Person, Group or Organisation A	Person, Group or Organisation B
1. Initial interaction *(What A does and says)* Brief script describing actions with script Add perception of OrgZoo Character displayed	**2. Initial Response to 1** *(What B does and says)* Brief script, actions and Add perception of OrgZoo Character displayed
3. Response to response *(How A reacts to B's response)* Brief script, actions and perception of OrgZoo Character displayed	**4. Next Response** *(How B reacts to A's counter response)* Brief script and perception of OrgZoo Character displayed
5. Next response *(Etcetera)* Brief script, actions and perception of OrgZoo Character displayed	**6. Next response** *(Etcetera)* Brief script, actions and perception of OrgZoo Character displayed *Additional exchanges can be added if desired.*

Figure 7.4.2. Template for planning a Behavioural Role-Play

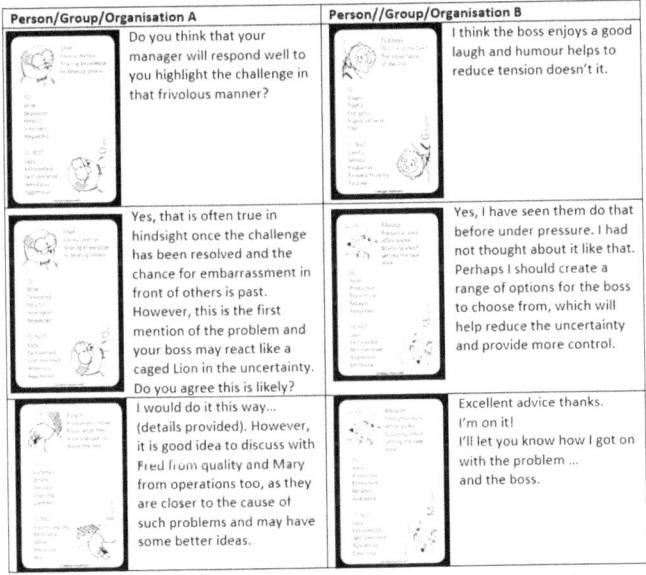

Figure 7.4.3. Example of a scripted role play using the Behavioural Role Play template

BECOMING ADAPTABLE

Insights

Outputs from any activities can be appropriately or inappropriately used by others if they are recorded. Remind participants to respect others' perspectives and shared insights, thoughts and feelings when facilitating and when reusing any examples or outputs from any interactions. Permission should always be secured before reusing or sharing any recorded output elsewhere. The Chatham House Rule (chathamhouse.org/about-us/chatham-house-rule) is a good guide on such matters.

The template is not necessary if people have a good scenario they wish to work on. Alternatively, the prompts can be written on a whiteboard or flipchart and the OrgZoo cards can be used on the tables to storyboard a scenario. Another creative way to produce the role-play is to ask participants to draw a small comic strip of activities and then describe them to the other groups.

I find acting scripts out as a play generates more fun and active feedback, but some people regard this kind of performance with horror. Always be aware of the preferences of your participants and provide a range of options whenever possible. Remember, some groups like a specific and clear process while others like some flexibility to inject their own personality into the process. They key is to get them to use the activity as a conversation starter and generate a flow of ideas around behavioural interactions.

More complex scripts with more actors in the scenario can be generated for greater insights if you have more time available. For example, adding third or fourth actors can show scenarios where a character can influence their ultimate target through other people. An example might be

7. Examples of facilitation activities

a political leak through a credible source to assess the reactions among wider stakeholder groups. This provides some feedback for refinement before the official plan's launch, after which it may be difficult to adjust. For such scenarios, simply add more columns for each additional actor in the script.

Activity 7.5 Behaviour Matching in Context

Relationships can be created or destroyed depending on how well behaviours are aligned or misaligned. One of the foundations of relationships is how well matched the participants believe their behaviours are. This does not imply having identical behavioural preferences, as matched behaviours can be different depending on the perceived roles in the relationship.

In balanced adult personal relationships, a high degree of same behaviours is appropriate as the two people involved are equals. However, some degree of flexibility is appropriate as each party takes on different roles in different situations.

In professional relationships, there are many examples of unequal situations. Some valid examples of unequal relationships include employee and supervisor, employee and 'skip manager' (one level above immediate supervisor), manager and owner, mentor and mentee. The behavioural expectations of these are in contrast to those of professional peers which theoretically, but not necessarily in reality, are more equal.

Being aware of the behavioural expectations in a variety of situations is important to get the balance right. Sometimes understanding the behavioural expectations helps to reinforce the strength of the relationship, thereby contributing to increased productivity and reduced stress. These outcomes are generated by each party in the relationship understanding and respecting how their behaviours match.

BECOMING ADAPTABLE

There are other situations in which the relationship expectations are unhealthy and unsustainable, so the behavioural mismatching can be rectified through deeper understanding of the situation. An example of this is bullying behaviour, where one party is misbehaving to take advantage of another. The perpetrators of such inappropriate behaviours may or may not be aware that their behaviour is inappropriate. Behavioural matching activities can assist to highlight the strengths and challenges of a situation and enable a constructive conversation to improve the situation.

Some situations are unrecoverable and relationship termination should always be considered as a viable option. In such cases, the behavioural matching activity can provide the reflective dialogue and evidence to highlight that withdrawal from the relationship is the best option for the target of the inappropriate behaviour. These activities alone should not be used to replace counselling or support services. They are a way to self-reflect or share your perceptions with a trusted confidant to enable the challenges to be understood and resolved when possible.

Relationships are highly complex arrangements that are not easily discussed by many people. Our behaviours reflect our sense of identity and worth. Challenging how someone behaves can be a very dangerous activity and must be done with great care. Problematic relationships may need the involvement of counsellors and perhaps even lawyers. However, slight misunderstandings where there is good will, or a relationship that is not evolving as one or the other expects, can often be adjusted with a good conversation. This could take the form of a constructive dialogue about the expectations from both parties using the Behaviour Matching In Context technique (perhaps with a facilitator to ensure an independent perspective on the situation). A version of the technique can also be used to pre-empt relationships with people or organisations that you would like to connect with (see the stakeholder assessment activity later in this chapter).

7. Examples of facilitation activities

Purpose

Behavioural Matching In Context provides a way to visualise behavioural exchanges in a relationship to enable deeper reflection on whether these are appropriate or not. This can assist a person to understand more deeply how to improve their relationship and guide the direction they would like the relationship to evolve towards.

The arrangement of the behaviours into short reflective scenarios enables the person to assess if they are matching or mismatching. This arrangement can be done as self-reflection, discussed with other trusted parties, or as a group activity with the other party in the relationship. The aim is always to generate mutual benefit and improve relationships, or in some cases highlight reasons to terminate unhealthy relationships.

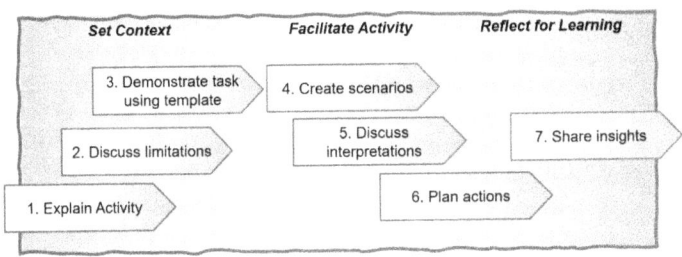

Figure 7.5.1 Overview of steps for Behaviour Matching in Context

Outputs

A series of scenarios (arranged OrgZoo character cards) to visualise behavioural exchanges between parties. These scenarios assist to describe the matches and mismatches in constructive conversations between parties.

Reflection notes about how to evolve or repair a relationship.

BECOMING ADAPTABLE

Outcomes

Stronger healthier, better balanced relationships.

Increased productivity, greater loyalty and elevated resilience.

Benefits

Greater awareness of the quality of the relationships and what impacts this.

Better relationships generate greater productivity and reduces stress.

Elevated awareness of the interdependencies between behavioural exchanges, their appropriateness, and the relationship outcomes.

Increased confidence to choose behaviours to enhance the relationship and reduce conflicts.

Beneficiaries

People involved in the relationships.

People who are impacted by the quality of the relationship between the parties.

Process

1: Explain activity. Explain that the activity involves using OrgZoo character cards to match behaviours in contexts. This involves representing a range of contexts in which the parties interact and highlighting the behaviour of each party in this context.

Scenarios used should be real situations that have happened, but anonymised.

Scenarios are kept to a single interaction, rather than a series as in role-plays (see template in Figure 7.4.2). However,

7. Examples of facilitation activities

multiple separate scenarios are useful to more completely characterise the relationships across a range of situations.

2: Discuss limitations. Discuss the limitations and dangers of openly discussing behavioural interactions between people. Even if anonymised people may identify who is involved, or assume they know who is involved and react negatively to the interaction.

This is a developmental exercise to improve the context for all in the relationship. It should not be done as a remedial activity to highlight the shortcomings of any person, but can be useful to get perspectives on how to deal with a challenging situation. Discussing actual behavioural interactions between specific individuals provides rich insights into the impacts of behaviour, but when we disclose such stories we need to act with the highest ethics and respect. The purpose of sharing insights is to find ways to improve the relationship or to help others who may have similar challenges.

Ensure that these points are acknowledged by the participants and that confidentially during the activity and beyond is assured. This is the ethical way to engage and anything less would be unprofessional.

3: Demonstrate task using template. Before the activity, take a good example of a completed template that is aligned with the expected scenarios. Walk through the example on the template, explaining that this is just an example and they should create their own in this format. Discuss this example with the participants, asking if they think the behaviours are matched for that relationship and context. It is a good idea to walk through one positive example (for example, a mentor providing support to a mentee) and one that is a challenged

BECOMING ADAPTABLE

relationship (like the scenario in the template). This shows that the activity can be used to understand matched and mismatched behaviours.

4: Create scenarios. Matching scenarios is best done in pairs or small groups. This is because the participants can socialise the situation to develop a deeper understanding for each other's perspectives. Encourage the creation of several behaviour matching situations, including positive relationships and some more challenged examples, to provide experience with a wider set of situations.

5: Discuss interpretations. Ask each group to share one scenario at first and to state whether they thought the behaviours were matched for that relationship. After each shared scenario, members of other groups can state what they thought about the matching. This may be disagreeing, agreeing, or adding some other insight from a similar experience they are aware of. Encourage dialogue around the scenarios before moving on to the next one. If a relationship is quite complex, it may be appropriate to share several scenarios together to get a more robust and complete sense of the relationship before the wider conversation happens. This takes longer to complete, but usually generates better outcomes.

6: Plan actions. The reasons for facilitating such discussions are to help people develop their own behavioural adaptability and to them find ways to improve relationships. This may be from good to even better, or from challenged to less stressed. The conversations are the first step in this process, but an action plan to change the relationship to a more a balanced, mutually beneficial one is an important output. Ideas for this plan are cocreated by the whole group sharing their thoughts on what they would do to positively influence the relation-

7. Examples of facilitation activities

ship. Even though these are anonymised scenarios and plans from one person's experience, they are often very useful for others who may have experienced similar relationship situations.

7: Share insights. Thank people for their participation and sharing, and ask them to highlight any insights they gained from the activity. This sharing of insights at the end of any activity can help others to broaden their own understanding as they can gain ideas that they did not get themselves during the activity.

Context of this scenario: Add a brief description to describe the situation and the nature of the relationship. For example: This is a professional Boss – employee relationship, situation is when new ideas are offered, they are always rejected without discussion.		
Person A	Person B	Impact
When person A wishes to engage in this context, they behave in this way…	The normal response from person B is to …	How this impacts Person A is…
Display OrgZoo character card to highlight how person A sees their own behaviour.	Display OrgZoo character card to highlight how person A perceives Person B's behaviour.	It may be appropriate to display one or more OrgZoo character card to highlight how person A would prefer person to behave.

Figure 7.5.2 Template for Behavioural Matching In Context

Insights

It is important to monitor the reactions in the room closely during this activity. Be very aware of any tensions developing and be prepared to pause or terminate the activity if there is any danger of the scenarios becoming dangerous.

This is an excellent activity in a professional group but, as always in dealing with behaviour, the environment needs to be well led to ensure psychological safety for all involved.

BECOMING ADAPTABLE

Some good questions to stimulate conversation around appropriate behaviours for a scenario are:

— Do you think it is fair for that person to behave that way in this context?

— How might Person A have achieved a better response than behaving the way they did?

— What do you think influences Person B to behave that way?

A team-forming version of this activity: an interesting, more gamified version of this to provide each participant a list of OrgZoo characters and assign them a dominant character of their own. Their task is to create a team of people based on their nominated dominant type for a specific purpose. The aim is to get them interacting in the room, socialising to meet and select people to form a diverse team that has matched behaviours that are aligned with the project aim (always acknowledging that a person is of course capable of all behaviours). As part of the team template, participants assess whether the people they meet in a specific character will collaborate, dominate or be neutral with them in that character. This activity highlights the limitations of looking at behaviours from a single perspective and emphasises that a diversity of behaviours is necessary for high team performance.

Activity 7.6 Stakeholder Assessment

There are always stakeholders for everything we do. A stakeholder is anyone impacted, positively or negatively, by the actions we plan to take. We can achieve better outcomes if we actively consider who these stakeholders are and what their stake in our activity is; that is, the nature of their interest in our planned activity (constructive or actively against our plan).

7. Examples of facilitation activities

When considering stakeholders, it is useful to think of their level of support for your activity (from strongly opposed, to the point of actively campaigning or acting against you, through to strongly supportive, and all possible positions in between). Remember also that their position can change during the implementation of your initiative and that this change can be influenced by the way you interact with them (or ignore/take advantage of them).

Stakeholders may be individual people, groups, organisations or government agencies. Clearly it is not possible to do a full stakeholder analysis on all of these on a regular basis. However, a complete list of all stakeholders should be created for any significant undertaking and monitored as appropriate.

Purpose

The aim is to understand the behavioural profile of your stakeholders, so that you can constructively engage with them to secure the best possible outcomes over the duration of your initiative.

Developing an understanding of the behavioural preferences of your supportive stakeholders helps you build stronger relationships. Understanding the behaviour of your opponents helps with decisions on how to mitigate the impacts they can have on your initiative.

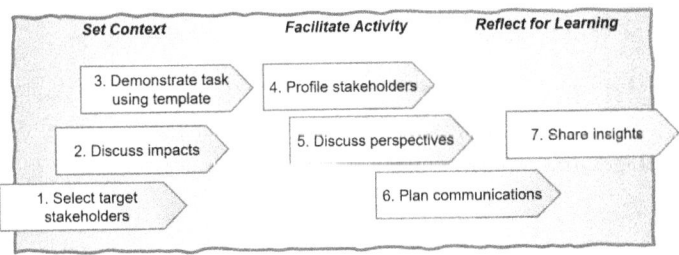

Figure 7.6.1 Overview of steps for Stakeholder Assessment

BECOMING ADAPTABLE

Outputs

A behavioural profile of your key stakeholders. This helps in developing stronger relationships with stakeholders though deeper understanding of their preferences.

List of stakeholders who support your initiative and those competing or advocating against it.

Reflection notes about the best ways to engage with these stakeholders.

Outcomes

Increased confidence in how to engage your stakeholders and mitigate against challengers.

Ability to quickly visualise likely behavioural exchanges with stakeholders.

Understanding where the matches and mismatches are between you and your stakeholders or challengers.

Ability to facilitate more informed conversations about stakeholder engagement plans.

Benefits

Stronger stakeholder relationships

Deeper understanding of competitors and challengers.

Ability to plan and implement effective stakeholder communications.

Beneficiaries

You and your team members.

Your stakeholders.

Your sponsors and customers.

7. Examples of facilitation activities

Process

1: Select target stakeholders. Discuss which stakeholders from your list you wish to create a behavioural profile for. Normally you would only do a behavioural profile of key stakeholders who may be supportive or a challenger to your initiative.

This assumes that you have listed, categorised and prioritised your stakeholders earlier. If not, look for approaches for creating your overall list of stakeholders (Shelley 2017).

2: Discuss impacts. Ask participants what types of impacts this/these stakeholder(s) have on your initiative.

Discuss how the behaviour of the stakeholders may vary with context or phase of your initiative.

Agree the stakeholders (individual or groups) you wish to profile. You may decide to select several stakeholders, with each one profiled by a different group.

3: Demonstrate task using template. Select one of the stakeholders from the list and have an open discussion about them, using the template.

If you have an earlier profile example that the participants are familiar with, this can be used to show them the output and the flow of the activity.

Go through the whole process, completing the profile and insights before breaking the participants into pairs or small groups.

Consider whether you want multiple perspectives of the same stakeholder in one context, or you want the same stakeholder in different situations, or each group to profile a

BECOMING ADAPTABLE

different stakeholder. All are valid, depending on what you wish to achieve.

4: Profile stakeholders. Each group uses the template to:

— Name the selected stakeholder and their impact/influence on the initiative

— Use OrgZoo cards to highlight how they predict the stakeholder may behave in the context

— Record insights about the stakeholder in column 3 to preserve the information for reuse.

5: Discuss perspectives. Ask each group to share the output and outcomes of their discussion about the stakeholder with other groups. This is done to firstly share what they have cocreated and secondly to gain some insights from others who may reinforce their findings or add other insights (which may include contradicting opinions).

6: Plan communications. Discuss how you can best engage with the stakeholder, based on how you expect them to behave (remembering it may be a behaviour that is not supportive of your initiative).

Build plans to communicate and engage with each stakeholder about the project in a way that is perceived to provide the best possible outcomes for all parties.

Sometimes there will be conflicts between stakeholders and this activity can help plan how to best to minimise the negative impacts.

Ensure the stakeholder profile and plan and any outputs are maintained as confidential documents.

7. Examples of facilitation activities

Context of this scenario:		
Add a brief description to describe the situation in which you are assessing the behaviour. **For example**, this stakeholder is supportive of our initiative – we want the stakeholder to become an advocate of our initiative when engaging with senior management.		
Stakeholder (in this context)	**Expected behaviours**	**Insights from the profiling conversation**
Name of the stakeholder or group being assessed and a few notes as to why they are important to your initiative.	Display OrgZoo character cards to highlight how you would expect this stakeholder to behave.	What does this profile suggest about matching behaviours to achieve the desired outcomes?
		Capture shared insights about the stakeholder to refer back to, especially useful if your profiling was not as expected.

Figure 7.6.2 Template for Stakeholder Assessment

7: Share insights. Ask if anyone would like to share insights before you move on. Reinforce the sensitivity of discussing the behaviour of others and the importance of respect and confidentiality for all parties.

Insights

Some participants may consider stakeholder profiling in this way politically or socially incorrect. This is not the case if the intent is to understand the stakeholder to build a positive and constructive relationship. It is true that profiling is inappropriately used by some people in some situations. For this reason, it is important to be very clear and transparent about the ethics of the process you are embarking upon. If there is any indication of people engaging in an unethical manner in this (or any) activity, it is the facilitator's responsibility to stop the inappropriate behaviour immediately and, if necessary, remove the offenders from the activity.

BECOMING ADAPTABLE

Activity 7.7 Exploring connected foundations of culture clash, innovation and cultural transformation

The most common outcome of a discussion about differences is argument or conflict. People often assume that if they are right, and you think differently, you must be wrong. This misses the great opportunity of mutual learning, as a range of possibilities can all be applicable in many situations.

The human world is highly subjective to each individual, and we come to believe the way we know is the right way. This often comes with the assumption that your way is the only way, or at least the best way. Familiarity with something that works adequately does not mean is it the best way forward, but many people cannot be bothered to find alternatives when they have an adequate solution. Often there is a wide range of approaches that can be applied to achieve desired outcomes in a given situation, with a variety of outcomes, some preferable over others.

For these reasons, collaborative conversations should always try to elicit a diversity of perspectives early in the dialogue. This can apply to physical things, but also to relationships and behavioural preferences. Creative options often emerge when differences are compared and understood at a deeper level. Adopting the best features of several options can be a strong driver of innovation and gets used in Agile project management and events like hackathons. The Creative Friction style of conversation enables constructive dialogue about differences in order to generate new possibilities. Done well, they can lead people to deeper understanding of each other and stronger relationships as well.

From cultural and personal development perspectives, we can learn a lot from comparing differences in our behavioural preferences or our cultures. One simple and inclusive way to compare culture is by contrasting the Behavioural DNA images of different cultures (or people) for the same context. A basic visual comparison of the patterns in Behavioural DNA images can be effective for most

7. Examples of facilitation activities

situations. Seeing where each character is selected reveals where the people agree and disagree about the appropriateness of that behaviour. Exploring these differences, and the reasons they exist, stimulates rich insights about how we act differently and why.

It is also possible to be a little more quantitative about the analysis. Selections can be scored to indicate whether the behaviour is considered appropriate/matched to the context:

+4 for expected/must have/mostly

+2 for desired/usually or inappropriate/mismatched

-2 for tolerated/not usually

-4 for rejected/rarely

This provides a basic numerical comparison of the perspectives of different cultures and how closely aligned they are for each of the behaviours. It is meant to be a conversation starter. Clearly the initial arrangement in the Behavioural DNA is subjective, not an absolute measure. As such the measurements should not be taken too far beyond just highlighting where the bigger and smaller gaps are. It is more to help people visualise the magnitude of the behavioural shift than a true quantitative tool.

This approach can also be used to assess the difference between the current state and a desired future state, informing a significant shift in culture over time. Figure 7.7.2 shows how this type of analysis can inform decisions around the types of behaviours that are encouraged and discouraged to achieve a cultural transformation. Cultural transformations are extremely difficult to achieve and rely on the willingness of people to engage in the program. The comparison of various visual representations of current and future behaviours helps people understand the shifts required to achieve the desired future state. Although no cultural transformation is easy, the conversations these images stimulate help bring people together on what can be achieved and how they need to adapt their behaviour to realise those changes.

BECOMING ADAPTABLE

Purpose

This technique can be used to simply combine Behavioural DNA images with subjective analysis to understand differences between cultures.

A more sophisticated application is to understand the differences between cultures through creative visualisations that enable comparison of behavioural profiles across cultures. These images stimulate conversations about desired behavioural shifts to enable a person, team or organisation to adapt their behaviour to an agreed future state. This enables participants to understand the sources of culture clash, the drivers of cultural transformation, and how these can be assets for creativity and innovation.

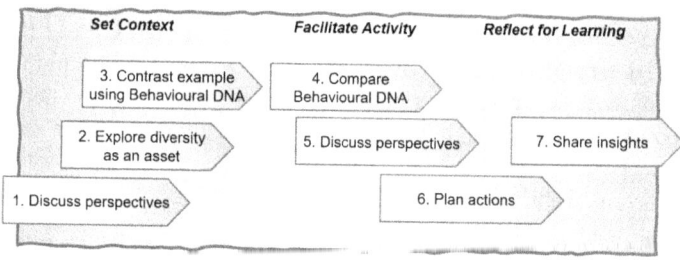

Figure 7.7.1 Overview of steps for Culture Clash and Transformation dialogue

Inputs

Behavioural DNA profiles of the cultures you want to compare, or the current and future states. (See Activity 7.2.)

People with an open mind and a desire to constructively contribute to culture change.

Time: understanding culture to build connections, collaboration or align change is not a simple one-off activity. It takes dedication and time invested with goodwill.

7. Examples of facilitation activities

Respect: without mutual respect and high ethical standards, these initiatives will not work and may even damage relationships.

Extreme care should always be exercised when dealing with differences of perspective and culture. However, with these in place and appropriate leadership, huge value can be achieved with the advanced applications of OrgZoo tools.

Outputs

A comparison of the differences between cultures (either visual or a numerical assessment).

A set of insights and actions to determine how to proceed to develop the relationships and culture in the desired direction.

Outcomes

Deeper understanding of your culture and of the comparison state (future or others').

Elevated ability to converse about behavioural differences.

Capability to visualise a culture as a set of behaviours.

Ability to cocreate and implement a set of actions to enable cultural transformation.

Confidence to engage in conversations about differences in culture and expect this to develop stronger relationships rather than conflict.

Greater resilience to adapt in multicultural environments and build mutual respect despite differences.

Benefits

Stronger relationships and commitment to cultural evolution.

BECOMING ADAPTABLE

Deeper understanding of how to implement cultural change.

Ability to plan and implement effective cultural communication.

Greater harmony and less stress and conflict.

Enhanced ability to resolve issues and find creative solutions for innovation.

More progressive and open culture based on mutual respect and ethical relationships.

Beneficiaries

You and those you interact with.

Everyone interacting with the cultures being assessed and their stakeholders.

Your employers, sponsors, partners, customers and consumers.

Process

1: Discuss perspectives. Given the importance and sensitivity of comparing people and cultures, strongly set the tone of the activity and expectation of ethical exchanges and mutual respect.

Highlight the value available from professionally engaging in exploring differences.

Share an example of where value was generated when people came together to stimulate ideas from different perspectives.

Explain that points of difference will usually generate conflict, unless the mindset is focused on understanding why these exist and the advantages of understanding how the differences could apply differently, or be combined to generate something new.

7. Examples of facilitation activities

2: Explore diversity as an asset. Highlight how a range of options and how they are applied is an opportunity to adopt an alternative approach.

Discuss how an exploratory (divergent) mindset is required to generate new insights.

Ask participants to share examples where an idea that was being used in one culture created value and changed behaviour in another (asking rather than telling is more likely to open minds and build confidence to engage in Collaborative Conversations).

Ask for an example where observing an idea or behaviour in another situation stimulated the participants to see it as an asset and act differently as a result.

Such examples and shared stories can be very simple; they do not need to be long, deep explanations. For example (just add the specific details), I always did my role in this way and then I saw a peer do something completely different. At first, I thought that was a bit crazy. However, after discussing it with them, it became clear to me that their way was more inclusive and productive. Since then, my relationships with my own team have strengthened and we have become more innovative.

3: Contrast example using Behavioural DNA. Take a previous example of a culture clash, a great innovation or transformation story, discuss the story behind it and the impacts it had.

There are several examples in this book and many publicly accessible articles about such moments that could be used.

BECOMING ADAPTABLE

Choose one that relates to your own planned comparison if possible.

Ask participants for their impressions of the outcomes and thoughts on how they would have approached the example differently.

4: Compare Behavioural DNA. Break into pairs or small groups. Determine if each group is making the same comparison.

Each group to select the two Behavioural DNA examples you wish to compare.

There are many states that can be compared, for example:

— Your assessment of your current culture and the desired future state

— What you think your culture is and what another party thinks it is

— Your culture and another culture (either as assessed by you or self-assessed)

Facilitate a discussion of the key similarities and differences between the two profiles.

Share perspectives about these differences and explore why they might exist

Make notes about the insights discussed and reflect on which ones are most important to share with other groups.

5: Discuss perspectives. Each group shares a short summary of their discussion to highlight what they think the key differences are and why these exist. The group then shares a short story or situation in which the differences have led to constructive outcomes when managed. It is okay to also have

7. Examples of facilitation activities

some groups share a story when this led to conflict, but make sure that there is a balance of positive outcomes to ensure participants are encouraged to leverage the differences as assets, rather than just reinforce differences as a source of conflict. A good way to leverage a negative outcome is to discuss how they could have created value if they had behaved differently.

6: Plan actions. Based on the insights, stories and reflections from the step 5 discussions, brainstorm (as small groups or a whole group) ideas on how to move forward, leveraging the differences as positive assets. A good way to generate these ideas is to use the Cocreated Projects Worth Doing approach (Shelley 2020a), describing all ideas and actions in the format of: Action, Descriptor, Subject, for a Purpose. These ideas and actions are then prioritised across the group to develop initiatives to enable the transformation to be implemented.

7: Share insights. Ask teams to reflect on their experiences of this activity and how they might use the process going forward. Shared perspectives help other participants to broaden the ways they might use the approach in future. This deepens the learning outcomes and builds their capabilities towards Becoming Adaptable.

In the example shown in Figure 7.7.2 the desirability of each behaviour is highlighted for the future culture the organisation wishes to transition towards. When the behaviours are displayed in this way (based on their own cocreated Behavioural DNA profile), they are more easily able to visualise the behaviours. These insights help the participants to discuss what types of projects and actions they can perform to enable the transformation.

BECOMING ADAPTABLE

Another way to visualise this is to compare the scores of the current culture with the future desired state and highlight the gaps. This was performed for a Singapore project organisation that was about to be disbanded. They cocreated a strategy for continuation based on these insights. A proposal was put to the parent organisation and the organisation was formalised into a permanent service provider. The organisation continues to be a key strategic player in the Singapore market several years later, which was enabled by this transformation.

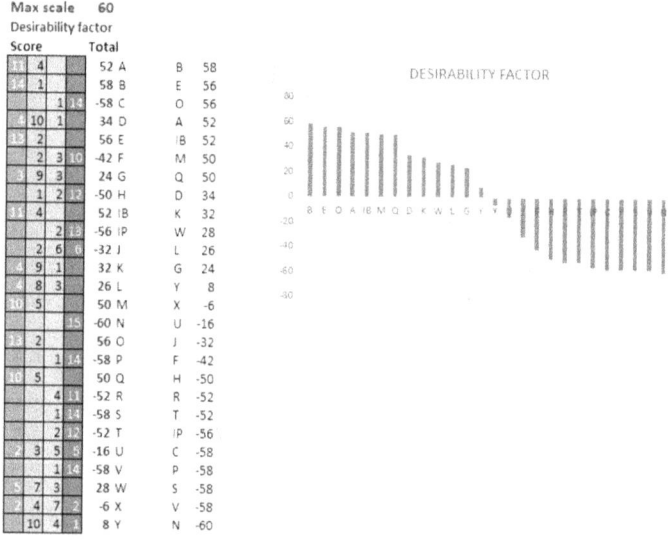

Figure 7.7.2 Example analysis of Behavioural DNA to highlight desirability of future behaviours.

8. Tools for efficiency and effectiveness

Behaviour is all about people and the way they interact. It is the foundation of culture and the basis of relationships in a connected society. So why include a chapter on tools in a book about behavioural adaptability? Let's explore that question…

There is a famous, and widely used, image of three concentric circles showing a sweet spot in the intersections of people, process and tools. These days, most people struggle to think of a tool that is not some sort of software application or other computer-based technology. In fact, a tool can be anything that enhances your ability to achieve your aim.

Variations of the three overlapping circles have been used in management for decades to highlight that effective actions requires people interacting with each other, though processes that generate value, supported by tools. Mostly the circles are the same size, which is a bit misleading as it suggests that each element is of equal importance. The three circles are often shown in different

BECOMING ADAPTABLE

configurations, which may also be misleading as it suggests that the order in which they are considered is not important.

My personal preference is shown in Figure 8.1. It highlights that people, including behaviour and culture, are at the apex with the other two as supporting elements. A good balance of process (getting things done effectively) and tools (ensuring what gets done is efficient, well captured for future learning, and measured) sets a solid foundation for the people aspects. This highlights the pre-eminence of people in delivering value, while acknowledging that good processes and tools will accelerate outputs and amplify outcomes.

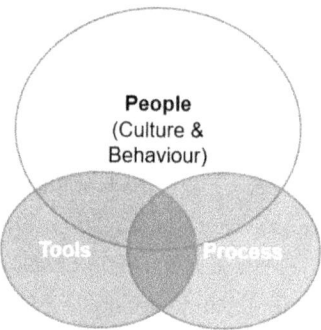

Figure 8.1 Harmonising relationships between people, process and tools for optimal outcomes

Each industry emphasises different parts of the diagram. In the software industry, the tools circle can inflate and bias the focus around the technological aspects. In government and critical risk industries, process tends to dominate to enable governance and control. However, without the best people, the very best processes and tools produce suboptimal results. In contrast, a great team can still generate useful outcomes by replacing good processes or tools with other qualities such as creativity, ingenuity and collaboration. How you harmonise your circles is a judgement call for the situations you face and the teams you engage with. In my

8. Tools for efficiency and effectiveness

experience, making sure your people are role models for behavioural adaptability helps them to align with purpose across various situations. This generates the best culture and outcomes.

Many useful tools are available to support teams and using a variety of these is good practice. However, despite people agreeing that behavioural adaptability is an important success criterion, there are not many processes and tools that focus on how to achieve *Becoming Adaptable*. This chapter shares insights on OrgZoo tools that have been refined over nearly 20 years to enable high-quality facilitation about behavioural adaptability. These tools continue to be evolved by practitioners and ambassadors and shared through OZAN.

OrgZoo character cards

The OrgZoo character cards provide a simple and kinaesthetic way to engage people in inclusive, constructive and psychologically safe conversations about behaviour.

The elements of play, social inclusion and cocreation are important aspects of the learning experience in *Becoming Adaptable*. The character cards act as neutral representations of behaviours, enabling exploration of different perspectives about their applicability across a range of contexts.

Each character card represents a behaviour, not a person. For example, Lion represents strong control and command and Bee represents collaborative team work. Twenty-five of the characters are based on animals and one on a plant (representing giving and to balance the ecosystem). There are two created characters (not real, Unicorn and X-Breed), and one that did exist but is now extinct (Triceratops). The characters were deliberately chosen to most effectively reflect the behaviour being portrayed.

The behaviour is typical of how most people would connect with the character in nature. Some characters may not be immediately

BECOMING ADAPTABLE

apparent to some participants, but people soon come to understand the representation with the supporting words on the card and through conversation with others. This is what happens in reality as well, since there are some behaviours that are also not immediately apparent to people in lived situations. Typically, when people do not understand what is happening, they observe, reflect more deeply and then talk with trusted peers to understand.

Seeing each behaviour as an object, independent of the people displaying it, depersonalises the conversation and allows the behaviour to be explored more deeply. In effect the characters become a miniature language that participants quickly learn (Shelley 2012). This enables participants to explore where the behaviour is aligned with the desired outcomes — and where it is likely to be misaligned and therefore a barrier. This reinforces that a person can display different behaviours in different situations (as discussed earlier in the book).

Each character card has an image of the plant or animal; five words that are strong, easily observable features of that character; and five words that are not typical. Understanding the wider nature of the character (behaviour) is an important aspect of being more behaviourally aware.

Using the OrgZoo Character cards is quite intuitive and people do not need much prior exposure to engage in most of the interactions described in Chapter 7. Starting with the cards, the participants can quickly build up a behavioural profile of anyone or any situation in which people can be observed to be interacting. The profile reflects the perspectives of the people involved and should not be considered an absolute answer. The activity should concentrate on the social exchange of understanding and perspectives between the people as mutual learning and relationship building. See Chapter 10 for a deeper discussion on the science behind the approach and Chapter 7 for descriptions of commonly-facilitated interactions (games) using the OrgZoo character cards.

8. Tools for efficiency and effectiveness

The cards are printed in English, Russian and German and there are translated guides in several languages including Mandarin, Vietnamese, French, Arabic and Thai. These guides are more context-specific than the language translation apps available for smartphones.

The OrgZoo Cards pack has two full A-Z sets of character cards, plus some support cards for other activities. The double set enables interactions of two groups comparing their perspectives of the same situation, or one group discussing two different situations (for example, now and future, or us and them). OrgZoo character cards are available directly from Intelligent Answers or OZAN Ambassadors.

Figure 8.2 OrgZoo character cards

Online profiler

The online profiler is a simplified way to explore the OrgZoo behavioural characteristics. A card-based activity starts with

BECOMING ADAPTABLE

arranging the characters to generate images and words describing a person, team or situation. The online profiler starts with arranging words into categories (taken from the complete descriptions of the OrgZoo characters {Shelley 2007}) to generate a profile of the characters most likely to fit that description. In effect, it is a reversal of how the cards operate.

From the OrgZoo profiler website, a person first identifies:

— who or what is being profiled (a person, a team, a situation)

— and the context in which it is being assessed (normal daily activities, in a crisis, current observation, future desired state etcetera

These entries do not affect the profile output and are not recorded in background: they are for the person generating the profile to identify the specific context in the report. This is important, as a person's behaviour does change across contexts. A generic profile of a person that does not recognise variations in different situations is more of a stereotype than a clear description of the person in context. Similarly, the report identifies whether the profile was completed as a self-assessment or by some external party. This will influence how it is interpreted in later discussion.

Consider the context very specifically. Be clear about what you are profiling, for example how you actually observe the behaviours or what you would like them to be. These are very different questions. People are variable in the way they act, depending on context and other influencing factors. Instead of terms like 'aways' and 'never,' which are absolute, try describing the most dominant or less common behaviours.

Once six words are entered into each of the four categories, the online profiler will generate a report. This can be used for:

— self-reflection

8. Tools for efficiency and effectiveness

— asking someone for their feedback on you or another person or group
— doing 360-degree feedback reviews for a group of people

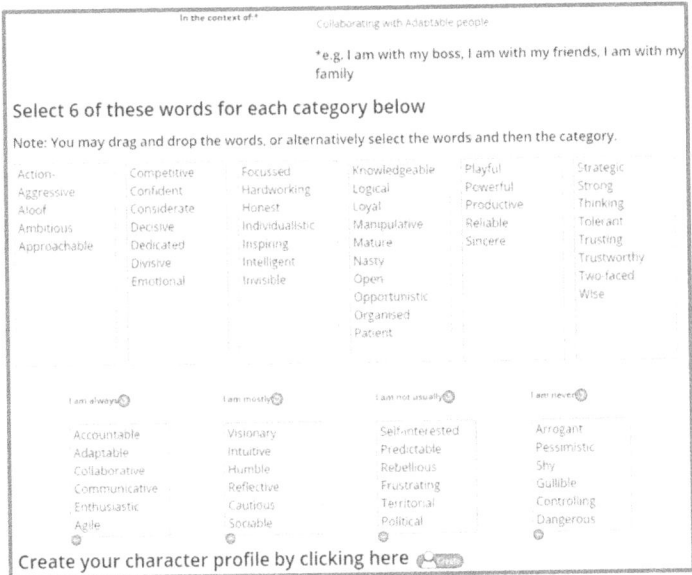

Figure 8.3 OrgZoo online profiler showing allocation of words to categories

In anonymous 360-degree profiles each person completes a profile of the people or team and sends the generated report to the facilitator. The facilitator compiles the profiles, anonymising the reports, and passes the result to the person or team being profiled, often with some summarising remarks. This can be a good way to get honest feedback from a range of colleagues on how they perceive your behaviour. Delivering constructive, honest feedback on the behaviour of work colleagues can be challenging in more direct face-to-face interactions, so this approach provides a convenient alternative.

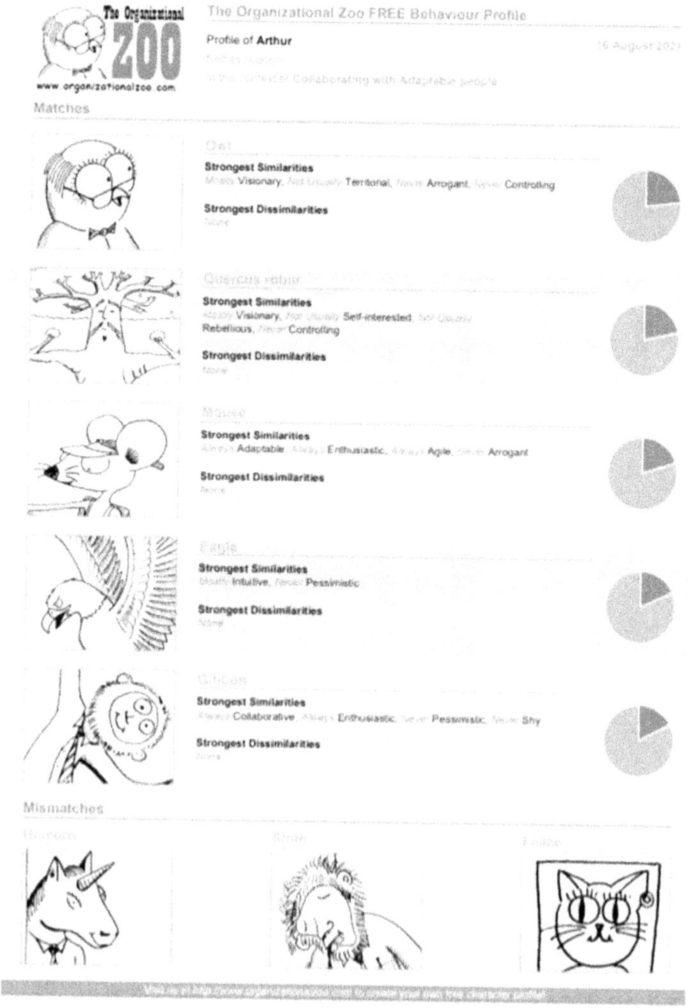

BECOMING ADAPTABLE

Figure 8.4 Example output from the OrgZoo behavioural profiler

8. Tools for efficiency and effectiveness

Figure 8.4 shows the output from the online profiler. Based on the words chosen in each of the four categories, the algorithm generates a similarity score between that combination of words and the profiles of all the OrgZoo characters.

The numerical result is calculated from the combination of matches (where the word appears in the same category or adjacent category, increasing the score) and mismatches (where the word appears in an opposite category, reducing the score), This results in the overall similarity score. The profile highlights the five closest and the three least similar characters to the recorded profile.

Conversations That Matter

The structure of *Conversations That Matter* is critically important to all OrgZoo facilitated activities.

The activities are built around stimulating shared perspectives through conversation to cocreate new possibilities, not to lead the participants to a prior defined answer. The tools, games and activities are what I refer to as conversation starters. The conversations are the process by which we learn and build relationships. The tools support and scaffold that conversation through to completion, but it is the conversation itself and the shared insights that generate the true learning and capability development. This social interaction, as the participants share and cocreate outputs, has them simultaneously experiencing the knowing, doing and being elements of learning.

Conversations That Matter are both an accelerator and a catalyst of the behavioural transformations that happen through OrgZoo interactions. Well designed and facilitated, they enable the participants to evolve through their own reflection and the feedback and insights from others.

Conversations That Matter are described in Chapter 6 and elsewhere.

BECOMING ADAPTABLE

Your mind, your mindset, and your behaviour

The most powerful tools in your possession are your mind, your mindset, and your behaviour. It is not possible to achieve success in any of this book's techniques if your mind is closed, your mindset is fixed, and your behaviour is not open to adaptation. Learning requires an investment of energy and persistence in your reflective practice. A facilitator needs to be a role model of what they are asking others to do in the activities. Learning and *Becoming Adaptable* occurs best when you understand the three challenges to self-improvement (Shelley 2018):

> It is not possible to
> LISTEN with your mouth open
> LEARN with your mind closed
> LEAD with a dispassionate heart

Listening and engaging in conversations is one of the most productive ways to learn and become adaptable. To become aware of something new to adapt yourself towards, you need to observe, discuss and practise it. Once aware of it, you can move through the four A's cycle (see Chapter 3) to become it. Your mind interprets what you observe in the world, which influences how you behave. The deeper you understand your own mind, the more likely you are to engage more constructively in your interactions with others. Meditation and scientific research demonstrate that it is possible to take more control of your mind. Meditation has been practised for centuries to help people settle the noise in their mind and to relax. it can also be used for observing and reflecting on behaviour. You often hear people say they did not have a choice, and in some cases they may be correct. However, I believe people generally have more choices than they realise. Training your brain to balance rational and emotional stimuli can contribute to greater resilience, which enables more conscious choice of behavioural responses.

Your mindset acts as a gatekeeper, influencing what your subconscious mind accepts and rejects. One reason for resistance to change is that

8. Tools for efficiency and effectiveness

your mindset simply rejects the proposition at face value, because it is outside the scope of your knowledge and experiences. Mastering your mindset is like mastering your mind. It requires practice. It is highly unlikely that you can become adaptable if you have an inflexible mindset. In fact, Becoming Adaptable often requires a shift in mindset, or at least acceptance that alternative possibilities are valid.

Behaviour is one of the most influential tools humans have. Children's behaviour influences their parents and other children. Business and life partners affect each other's behaviour and the quality of the relationship. Everyone behaves... You cannot unbehave, although you may have to apologise for a poor behavioural choice in retrospect. Behaviour is a powerful tool. The more you know how to use it well, the more likely you are to achieve your objectives. This can happen regardless of whether your objective is to help others or to inappropriately manipulate them.

One function of the OrgZoo Ambassadors Network is to ensure that behavioural capabilities are applied in ethical ways that contribute to mutual value creation. If you believe in karma, you may think that perpetrators of poor behaviour will eventually fail. Unfortunately, despite our favourite fictional stories, life does not always work out that way.

Video guides

Short video guides are available for the techniques in this book and some other OrgZoo techniques. The videos introduce the techniques but do not describe the full detail of how to facilitate the activities. The best way to develop capability and understanding of any of the techniques is to first watch these videos, then have a Conversation That Matters with an OZAN Ambassador where you share insights and expectations about how the activities can be facilitated.

BECOMING ADAPTABLE

Frequently asked questions (FAQ)

A list of frequently asked questions is available to OZAN members through the online knowledge base. While useful, the FAQ list is less valuable than face to face conversations with an OZAN Ambassador. There is no such thing as a generic situation with behaviour, so conversations with experienced practitioners tend to generate superior outcomes. Everything about behaviour is complex and the nuances need to be sorted through with deep reflection.

OrgZoo is not a counselling method nor a psychological advisory method. It is a tool to enable personal and professional development around behavioural awareness and adaptability. It can be a useful way to visualise behavioural situations and develop a mutual understanding of complex human interactions.

Smartphone app?

Ever since smartphone applications became available I have been tormented by the thought of developing one for OrgZoo. Given some of the insanely random apps that achieve great success and the vast number of apps available, I have always steered away from publishing one. At one stage OrgZoo Ambassadors Network members experimented with what could be achieved with an app.

Most of the value for people applying the OrgZoo concept comes from the social interactions that are stimulated by the games played. The game itself is just a catalyst for the learning. Screen-based interactions allow less nuance in the exchange of perspectives. There are some advantages, such as easy access to the character descriptions in a range of languages, and perhaps enabling virtual interactions more productively. However, so far the cost-benefit of investing in app development has not been high enough to warrant proceeding. We remain open to collaborate with a partner on creating an app, if there is mutual value in doing so, and if it delivers a positive learning experience.

SUCCESS STORY
Facilitating behavioural conversations in IT development

AJ Dulaney Shaw,
OZAN Ambassador, Australia

Context (where and when)

Why do we recognise that someone is important to an organisation when that person is inspiring, iconic or part of the brand, such as Barack Obama or Richard Branson. Yet at a project level, we often lose sight, or potentially devalue, the influence people have on team colleagues and project outcomes.

Why?

Stimulating deeper conversations about behaviour can engage people to understand the importance they play on perspectives and relationships.

Who?

Agile-like philosophies do emphasise a critical point, and that is we need more emphasis on people over process. Yet this perspective of being people focused is often implemented in the same way process enhancement methodologies are rolled out. That is as a cookie-cutter solution that is expected to deliver specific deliverables. This misses the point, because wherever people are involved, expect the unexpected.

What?

I've had great success with the OrgZoo character cards when rolling out a new business process. For example, implementing a continuous improvement initiative across IT departments. I ask the team to lay the cards out to reflect how they feel the existing

BECOMING ADAPTABLE

team is behaviourally. It is important to encourage them to do this task quickly, to get an instinctive view. This emotional sense of the team culture is more important than attempting to develop a considered, absolute assessment. This is because people act instinctively in these subliminal queues in the real interactions. This perspective stimulates authentic reflections on the cultural makeup for the whole group. This will influence the outcomes of your new processes.

I ask the team members to consider the individual behaviours and how over time they contribute to the flow of knowledge amongst the team, or act as a subtle blockage. If the team is larger, or you having difficulty picking where boundaries of the team lay, think within the context of a culture quadrant in the image below.

	Personal		
	People focused - Reflective		
Reality Closed Convergent	**Collaboration**	**Cultivation**	*Possibility* Open Divergent
	Control	**Competence**	
	Impersonal		
	Goal focused		

Framework adapted from Schneider's Culture Model (The Reengineering Alternative, 1999).

It can be useful to use each section to prompt yourself with questions about where observed behaviours do and do not fit.

Conversations around which behaviours are exhibited regularly and how these behaviours change when interacting with others trigger shifts in the team dynamics. These interactions often highlight insights like the influence the environment has on our behaviour. This can highlight the influences of organisational structure, departmental culture, or key stakeholders outside the team.

How? (did OrgZoo activities help)

When pitching a new process like continuous improvement, I dilute terminology by talking in layman's terms. If terminology is adopted before the new behaviours start forming, the end result may be people talking without the walking. I facilitate a conversation around what I call a 'buddy system', which is where colleagues have the opportunity assess one another's work and provide feedback. In the IT development field, I refer to this as 'back each other up, before software is released'. It is important to emphasise that software bugs and making mistakes are OK, it is how we handle our mistakes that makes us who we are. Your role as a facilitator of change is to provide a safe environment where the team can form around a process they will own.

Outputs (tangible short-term value delivered)

The immediate outputs of these workshops are improved program design and team performance. Team members are better connected through reviewing each other's work and this develops stronger relationships leading to better quality algorithms with less bugs. The OrgZoo characters start to embed as new language and approach to discuss challenging behaviours. Team members can refer to the OrgZoo characters to discuss a behaviour and this reduces the conflicts by enabling the behavioural challenges to be discussed before they create damage.

Outcomes (intangible long-term value delivered)

Participants in these workshops have found the conversations easier and more engaging that what they typically encounter in

BECOMING ADAPTABLE

IT. They better understand the impacts the behaviours have on the way software is designed and used, from a people perspective. They realise they benefit when they invest in new ways to be inquisitive about themselves and the people they collaborate with. One benefit of using the OrgZoo characters is that everyone remains anonymous. Talking in the third person depersonalises the behavioural discussions. This lowers the defensive aspects and opens participant's perspectives to adopt new ideas.

I have found the OrgZoo is a habit-forming tool, that with a little exploration can help us travel a long way towards understanding ourselves and those around us. I find the imagery instinctive in the way that I think about past and upcoming interactions. The OrgZoo characters help me identify peoples' individual behaviours, as and when they are happening, and when reflecting on how I might be perceived.

Part C

Theories and philosophies behind this approach

BECOMING ADAPTABLE

9. The Organizational Zoo

A brief history of OrgZoo time

I reflected on this book, *Becoming Adaptable*, for over a decade before daring to complete it.

My earlier book, *The Organizational Zoo*, was written between 2003 and 2006 and finally published in 2007. At that time there were only a few basic activities tested in practice. The book largely focused on defining the characters and exploring the promise of how the technique could be applied and would evolve with use. Even in 2007 I knew there would one day be an *OrgZoo Guidebook* of some sort.

Since the release of *The Organizational Zoo*, many additional ways to use the OrgZoo (as it has affectionately become known) have been successfully developed and applied to stimulate relationships, create opportunities, reduce stress and conflict, and enable people to interact more constructively in a wide range of contexts.

BECOMING ADAPTABLE

Here we are, fifteen years later, and *Becoming Adaptable* is finally published. If I had written this book in 2006, it would have been quite basic. Only one of the seven applications in this book existed at that time. Over the years since OrgZoo, practitioners and ambassadors have played with a range of ways to use the concept. Many of those workshops had diverse groups of participants and this added nuance to the perspectives of both facilitators and participants.

Using creative metaphor for understanding behaviour

The OrgZoo started as a small number of metaphorical characters to engage people in safely exploring the impact of behaviour on team relationships and performance.

Initially a few images of animals were used to characterise certain behaviours. Rather than talk about a person, the participants could exchange views about an individual behaviour exhibited by that person. The idea was to enable team members to talk openly about which types of behaviour were appropriate or inappropriate in a range of contexts. The animal characters gave a representational label for the behaviour, rather than using words that can easily be misinterpreted.

As the techniques were explored further, by me and other facilitators working in a range of contexts, a set of commonly observed characters (behaviours) emerged. A plant was added to represent giving and philanthropy. All animals consume, so to enable the possibility of a harmonised ecosystem some production of food and shelter was needed in the OrgZoo.

Determining the number of characters in the complete OrgZoo was challenging. After many iterations, we settled on a set of 27 characters. Firstly, this represents the behaviours found in a typical organisation, from the top (most strategic and controlling) to the bottom (most tactical) and from the most passive to the most

9. The Organizational Zoo

aggressive. Secondly, as there are 26 letters in the English alphabet, and one character for each letter, the zoo is easy to recall: A is for Ant, B is for Bee, et cetera. The letter Z for Zoo represents the behavioural ecosystem as a whole. Each character is designed to be recognisable for its behaviour in nature.

Over the years it became clear that different cultures recognise the behaviours quickly, but don't always agree on which behaviours they like to see displayed in various situations. Therefore, by organising characters in layers of preference, we can create a profile of a specific culture. This insight led to the creation of Behavioural DNA, an activity that enables groups of people to quickly cocreate their own assessment of what the observable behaviours are in their behavioural ecosystem. The Behavioural DNA activity is described in Chapter 7, along with a variety of other ways to engage people in constructive and inclusive conversations about behaviour.

OrgZoo today

The OrgZoo concept has been applied in twenty countries to engage people in constructive conversations about behaviour. This unique approach has generated amazing outcomes for the people involved, and in some cases changed their lives.

OrgZoo has worked for space exploration teams at NASA and aeronautics researchers in the United States of America.

In creativity conferences in Canada and Thailand.

Banking employees in Malaysia.

Local communities, learning and development institutes, and facilitator societies in Singapore.

Hotel employees in Bangladesh.

Knowledge sharing workshops in Saudi Arabia.

Knowledge managers in South Korea.

BECOMING ADAPTABLE

Leadership in Dubai.

Knowledge and collaboration society in South Africa.

Consultants in Vietnam.

Entrepreneurs in Russia and Brazil.

Social development professionals in Switzerland and Indonesia.

Environmental management in China and India.

University lecturers and students in Scotland.

Business leaders in England.

Innovators in Sweden.

In Australia it has been used in every sector; large, medium and small commercial companies; not-for-profit and government; education at primary, secondary, tertiary and executive postgraduate levels. In commercial executive education, OrgZoo has been applied in courses on leadership, entrepreneurship, human resource strategy, innovation, knowledge management, banking, government support services, learning, education, project management, real estate, health, construction, problem solving, and performance management.

OrgZoo Ambassador Network

Since the concept of the OrgZoo was created in 2004, it has evolved into a complex set of activities and games. It has stimulated deeper and more meaningful *Conversations That Matter.*

The OrgZoo Ambassador Network (OZAN) is a small international community who collaborate to share the OrgZoo concept and how it can be applied to create greater understanding of behaviour.

Members of the network are practitioners using OrgZoo techniques and who have engaged in a masterclass to learn the foundational techniques. Involvement as a member at practitioner level is

9. The Organizational Zoo

voluntary and by request. Trained practitioners who join OZAN are expected to facilitate OrgZoo activities at the highest ethical standard. They are encouraged to share their learning through a common portal and to engage with other members to further develop ideas using the OrgZoo concept.

OZAN membership is free and the philosophy of contributing to the community is embedded into how we interact. The members of OZAN are role models for *Becoming Adaptable*. Each member is a passionate advocate for the approaches used and the results these achieve for the communities they serve.

OZAN members continue to learn at a rapid rate as we collaborate with each other to find and cocreate new ways of applying the OrgZoo techniques. We share these insights so that you too can join in cocreating a better world, one in which we choose how to behave across a range of situations and achieve the best outcomes for all involved.

OZAN is dedicated group of people who love interacting around learning games and are passionate about making a positive difference for other people. Network members maintain a growing set of online support resources for active registered practitioners. Details about OZAN membership can be found online (organizationalzoo.com). Some stories of success for OZAN members are shared in this book so that you can see what can be achieved.

OrgZoo Practitioners

OrgZoo Practitioners are people trained in the use of OrgZoo techniques through the Practitioner Masterclass. These interactive learning programs are best experienced as face-to-face engagements but can also be facilitated online.

OrgZoo Practitioner training is necessary to comprehend the depth of the concept and gain experience of the basic techniques.

BECOMING ADAPTABLE

Practitioners are expected to facilitate activities to the highest ethical standards and ensure their participants receive a safe and enjoyable learning experience.

During the masterclass the dangers of poor facilitation, especially in the way behaviours are discussed, are highlighted as a critical component of the OrgZoo approach. The expectation is that practitioners will engage in responsible use of the techniques, but it is beyond the resources of OZAN to monitor all activities of all members. Practitioners reported to be acting unprofessionally will be removed from the registered practitioners listing.

OrgZoo Ambassadors

Some members of OZAN are honoured with title of Ambassador in recognition of their being an advocate of the OrgZoo approach over a long period of time and making many contributions to the community.

Ambassadors mentor OZAN practitioners and actively use and evolve the concept in their professional practice and personal lives. You can read the profiles of ambassadors on the OrgZoo website (organizationalzoo.com).

Stories of impact from OrgZoo interactions

Humans are natural story tellers. We learn from stories and we enjoy listening to them. Stories are a central part of all human cultures and are a traditional way of learning social aspects such as values, ethics, relationships and morals. All significant social initiatives are surrounded in stories because, like metaphor, they simplify what happened into digestible pieces and bring the application of the concept into reality.

Several short stories from OZAN members are shared throughout this book. Each story appears in a format aligned with the OrgZoo design and facilitation approach: why, who, what, how, and

9. The Organizational Zoo

outcomes. This should help you to connect the activities with the value cocreated in context of the organisation.

There are many more stories that can be told and the best way to get value from them is listening and conversing with OZAN community members in person (virtually or face-to-face). This is not selling — it is sharing and collaborating! Our collective experiences to help you to build behavioural awareness and accelerate you to become adaptable. We know it works through our own experiences and we are sharing those with you to help you in your journey.

BECOMING ADAPTABLE

SUCCESS STORY
Building behavioural adaptability in construction

Tom Blair,
OZAN Ambassador, Australia

Context (where and when)

Australia's largest volume home builder, with over A$1 billion in sales, was faced in 2011 with a challenge. How do they manage growth while continuously improving their market share, staff qualifications, customer satisfaction, and building upon their customer-centric culture.

Why?

There was strong competition for capable people to deliver projects in a highly competitive market with increasing client expectations. Those who can lead this environment attract the best customers and deliver into the most valuable part of the market. In doing so they generate a strong reputation and a solid commercial return for investors.

Who?

The strategy adopted and led by the General Manager of People and Business Improvement was to generate a positive culture, with a strong emphasis on customer expectations. Promoting and hiring quality staff that fit the culture was key, along with a new approach to training to increase the capabilities of staff. The design and implementation of a program to achieve this was put to tender. A leading university with strong workplace credentials submitted a proposal with appropriate scope and that was innovative, inclusive and bespoke. The proposal included more than just contextualising the training, it extended the design to embed key staff within the building company to fully understand the company's culture and the challenges that were being addressed.

The program designer and lead facilitator of the program invested time with company management and staff to understand the challenges and worked with the team to cocreate a unique, customised program. The Certificate IV in Building and Construction (Building) was created to meet the Australian Qualification Framework requirements and included a Zoo workshop to address behaviour in various areas of the program.

What?

The Organizational Zoo element that was developed within the training program was also specifically designed the cohort profile, specifically the site managers. Most of the participants did not hold any tertiary qualifications and mainly were promoted through from trades experiences.

How? (did OrgZoo activities help)

The workshops focused on customer relationships and team building within the home construction environment. Teams performed Behavioural DNA on different types of stakeholders they had engaged with, making the learning real and relevant for them. What occurred was truly transformational with the overall program, and the success of the program was measurable through increased productivity and strengthened relationships.

Outputs (tangible short-term value delivered)

The implementation of this people and capability strategy resulted in improved customer satisfaction based upon the net promoter score, improved build times and revenue.

Site managers received externally certified Certificate IV qualifications.

Outcomes (intangible long-term value delivered)

A culture of collaboration and improved behaviour was observed as more cohorts were graduated through the program. Company leadership acknowledged that OrgZoo integrated well

BECOMING ADAPTABLE

with other program elements and was a significant contribution factor to the success. This program broke new ground in training and change management in construction, delivering positive results in the company organisational culture and knowledge and skills of the staff involved. The company and the university, together with the Building Leadership and Simulation Centre (BLSC), provided clear metrics that demonstrated the value generated. The program quality was recognised by receiving some highly regarded industry awards up to being a national finalist. Many of the original participants in the program have now risen to higher levels of management within the company and continue to contribute to the company maintain its position of number one builder in Australia.

10. Theories embedded into OrgZoo philosophies

It's fun, practical and yet academically sound

Have you ever watched young children learn? They are amazing! Open mind, full of curiosity, not afraid to offer a suggestion, engaged with each other to explore in a divergent and experimental manner. They are full of critical analysis and questions. If the sign says "wet paint," they touch the surface to confirm. They collaborate to cocreate a range of plausible options (and several creatively implausible ones), which they test out through play. If someone does something crazy, they all have a good laugh. It is magical and fascinating to watch. They have so much fun learning…

Until formal education comes along and disrupts their natural instincts.

As a child I enjoyed school because my mind was like a sponge. I shared and explored ideas with others. What I found, and later as an adult reflected on deeply, was that the education system was so competitive and quantitative. We fell into the trap of content-based

BECOMING ADAPTABLE

teaching, often out of context. Teaching facts may be academically sound and easiest to measure objectively; however, it does not produce well-adapted people who are ready to engage constructively in the real world. It is neither the natural nor the optimal way to learn.

Through my own professional practice, I learned that bringing playful and social elements into workplace interactions inevitably enhanced performance. Facilitated this way, people wanted to be there because it was both useful and fun. In contrast, pushing people into mandatory training sessions is often seen as either an excuse for 'time off work' or a drudgery, or both. I am not the only one who thinks there are better ways to build capabilities. The late Sir Ken Robinson, for example, was highly a respected educator with strong views on bringing creativity and social interaction back into formal education. (Robinson 2016)

The practitioner and academic literature is full of articles highlighting the benefits of social, problem-based, collaborative and student-centred learning, and yet these practices are not the mainstream. Why is it so hard to change the patterns of educational habit? The good news: there is growing momentum behind ideas that align with more interactive and social ecosystem learning (Ogden 2017) — we just need to grow the movement and persist!

How do we create academically sound social learning experiences that build relevant capabilities for personal and professional development? This is especially critical as the world changes so quickly. We need to be constantly learning new things to remain relevant and productive. The concept of lifelong learning is morphing into lifestyle learning, recognising that people benefit from incorporating learning into their lifestyle as a natural part of their daily activities (Shelley and Goodwin 2018). People enjoy the flexibility of microlearning — a short video on a topic of immediate relevance to them whilst commuting or just in time before a critical conversation. This is how we are evolving to learn, but with this

10. Theories embedded into OrgZoo philosophies

convenience comes the possibility of compromised quality. Reflecting on a short conversation starter (a short prompt for learning, for example a reading, a video, a quiz) is limited to your own interpretation. You can get richer insights and deeper learning if your understanding of the resource is shared in conversation with others. This provides a wider and deeper understanding and is more fun to discuss as this is the natural way for people to learn.

Becoming Adaptable is a type of learning: we learn more about behaviours and the situations in which they are most productive. The principles of social applied learning ecosystems apply here too. The deeper you understand each behaviour, and the more you discuss others' interpretations of them, the faster you can become adaptable.

As a form of learning, *Becoming Adaptable* also benefits from practice and reflection on that practice. Social exchanges and feedback with trusted partners and fellow learners accelerate this progress and are enjoyable to engage in. We all feel more committed to an endeavour when we have supportive partners collaborating with us on the journey.

Most humans are social creatures who are more likely to succeed as a collective than as individuals. The adage "If you want to go quickly, go alone. If you want to go far, go together" provides an insight worth acting on. Incidentally, pearls of wisdom like this offered as proverbs get bounced around everywhere and attributed to a range of famous people (Tolentino 2016). The important point is the concept of collaboration as a richer, more meaningful (and fun) way forward.

Scientific proof?

People often ask what evidence I have to prove these ideas are right. OrgZoo is neither a theory nor a model. It is an approach that stimulates learning. There is nothing to prove, other than whether OrgZoo helps people to better understand behaviour and its impli-

BECOMING ADAPTABLE

cations. I am not claiming it is a provable formula; just a good set of practices that enable you to make better behavioural choices. When Galileo discovered the existence of several celestial bodies using a telescope and mathematical calculations, he could prove they existed. That is, there was something in the sky that could be predicted from the patterns of motion around the sun. However, the future you does not exist yet. Future you (or us, if you are in a team or organisation) is something that you create yourself by the behavioural choices you make. It is not possible to prove a future social state, because there is no evidence of that state until you create it.

What I do claim for OrgZoo and *Becoming Adaptable* is that using these techniques will enable you to make more conscious choices about what the future you will be. The interactions, games and social reflection processes are adaptations of approaches that are used in professional practices in many fields (see the Appendix). Adding zoo metaphors just makes these approaches more engaging, easier to remember, and more practical for people who are not professionals in design thinking, coaching, facilitation and other fields.

Taking ideas and practices from a range of fields can generate synergies that people of all levels of education can apply. Generally during OrgZoo activities the supporting theories are not explained. Participants just engage in an activity that works for them. Sometimes people ask why it works, which is what this chapter explains. The OrgZoo Ambassadors' stories throughout this book offer examples of interactions, to provide a sense of what can happen when they are well facilitated.

How do we ever truly know anything? Where does knowledge come from? And how do you know it is truth? The best way is to do what children do — test it! Allow yourself to engage in some play with the concepts and see if it works for you. If it does, do more of it; if it does not help you, try something else.

10. Theories embedded into OrgZoo philosophies

The OrgZoo Ambassadors and Practitioners have facilitated many activities in many places with a range of participants. It is extremely rare for someone to say they did not enjoy the activities and learnt something from them. Trying something novel does require you to hold an open mind and build up the confidence to experiment beyond your comfort zone. Chatting to Ambassadors and Practitioners will enable you to determine whether the *Becoming Adaptable* approach is likely to be useful to you.

Each person is the sum of their experiences, knowledge, networks, and eagerness to learn. Some people have an insatiable passion to learn everything they can and apply this learning throughout their life. Others are happy to learn a few things and focus on this as a deep expert, sometimes rigidly. Some learn by believing what they are told without questioning it; others need to question everything they hear, gather evidence, and personally experience it before they can know it to be true.

There are many people who believe in things that simply do not exist (or that you do not believe exist). Who are we to tell them they are wrong and we are right?

The most important aspects of being human are intangible. They are not easily measured or proven. You cannot quantify the love two people feel for one another. You can observe the way they interact and draw some conclusions, but you cannot prove their love in a scientifically measurable way. Are your subjective observations and beliefs equivalent to proof? It seems to be sufficient evidence for many people to make life-changing decisions on.

That said, the OrgZoo and *Becoming Adaptable* approach takes into consideration a lot of scientific, social, business and psychological insights.

As a qualified scientist (Bachelor of Science and Master of Science), I have a strong preference for evidence and critical analysis. I deliberately assess the credibility of what I am observing and what I am told.

BECOMING ADAPTABLE

As a qualified social analyst (PhD in soft skills in teams) I am sensitive to, and respectful of, the differences people hold. As a qualified learning facilitator (Graduate Certificate in Tertiary Learning and Teaching) I know that interacting with people in social games accelerates their learning, but it may be a considerable time before they realise what they have learnt. The nature and sensitivities of these interactions are important to the learning experience and each person will read the situations differently. Some can be highly sensitive to comments or approaches, while others can be frustrated with too much emphasis on political correctness.

As a human, I am aware that my intent can be misinterpreted by others. This is why we must constantly be reading the room to gather and interpret feedback when engaging with others. We have many ways of viewing what we do and why. In my experience, assessing from a range of perspectives provides better options more often.

Human interactions are subjective and open to different interpretations. One person's truth is another's lie. Our truths are based on our own limited set of experiences. It can be hard to accept that something you are absolutely know as a fact is different from what someone else knows as their fact. It is possible that you are both right — or that you are both wrong.

Human knowledge changes as we learn more. What we thought to be true is often found, after a time, to be untrue. When Galileo published mathematical evidence that supported Copernican heliocentrism (asserting that the sun was the centre of the solar system and Earth travelled around the sun), he was subjected to an Inquisition and charged with suspicion of heresy. Galileo remained under house arrest for the rest of his life. Being right, but the dissenting voice against known truths, can require more than evidence!

Socrates too was treated poorly for attempting to open minds. He was more interested in stimulating arguments to seek out diversity

10. Theories embedded into OrgZoo philosophies

of views through argument than he was in commonly accepted assumptions and predefined answers. He too was tried and eventually executed for corrupting the minds of young people.

The state of knowledge about nuclear science and how it can be used for energy or warfare is less than 100 years old. Our knowledge of the structure of DNA and how it works is even younger. Mapping of the human genome was completed a scant 20 years ago. Artificial intelligence and machine learning are only just starting to emerge into useful disciplines, and we have not yet solved the complexities of designing such systems. Humanity is learning fast and we need to be open-minded and adaptable to ethically and appropriately apply these new insights.

Figure 10.1 Limited perspectives can create unnecessary conflicts

Our knowledge is always limited. Our systems of government and ethics do not keep pace with the creation of new knowledge. We constantly make decisions with limited understanding. Governments and organisations are not equipped to take every person into account: every decision taken on our behalf is a compromise. Some people react by withdrawing into themselves; some become activists to advocate for a specific way forward; and

BECOMING ADAPTABLE

others rebel against the system, through either peaceful social disobedience or violence.

So who is right and who is wrong? Is there such a thing as right and wrong? Are they opposite positions, or can opposites be parallel truths? Figure 10.1 demonstrates how different answers can be completely true. This figure appeared on the internet several years ago and had been adopted and adapted by many people to stimulate conversation and insights. It shows the power of simple visualisation can have to highlight an important point.

While Figure 10.1 highlights the limitations of a single perspective, it too is an oversimplification. The illustration only shows two perpendicular (opposing) perspectives of a simple three-dimensional inanimate object. However, a full sphere of 360 degrees is possible and the object can be more complex. When one circles the full sphere to see a more complex shape from many angles, there are many possible interpretations of the observed object. If there are infinite possibilities with just an inanimate object, imagine the possibilities when we look at all angles of complex social interactions!

Figure 10.2 Multiple perspectives can generate many perspectives to explore

10. Theories embedded into OrgZoo philosophies

Figure 10.2 shows another 3D shape casting multiple 2D shadows — yet some of those possible shadows simply are not possible in the real world. This is true also in human social and political systems. Self-interest, political influences, economic rationale, cultural nuances all influence what possibilities are proposed. Some alternative options are brilliant and worth investing in, whereas others are not possible (yet, perhaps). Some are for the benefit of the few at the expense of the many. Some alternatives are not sustainable.

This is where our critical thinking, leadership capabilities and adaptability are essential. The ability to decipher the various social, ethical, political, economic, legal, environmental and technological implications of a wide range of options seems daunting. We cannot tackle all choices this way, but it is worth applying deep analysis to life's big decisions. The quality of the options we adopt or adapt determines who we become and whether we are successful. It influences our reputation, respect and sense of self, in our own eyes and in the judgement of others.

Another important aspect of proof is that when we discover or create new knowledge it often replaces old knowledge. We must unlearn what we know, however reluctantly. Changing your mind too easily on important factors can make you gullible and therefore easily taken advantage of. Equally, we do not benefit from being so fixed in our views, knowledge and behaviours that we can never change anything once learnt. The world is constantly changing, which is why adaptability and open-mindedness are critical to ongoing success.

The following sections briefly describe what primary and secondary concepts have been designed into, or influenced, the OrgZoo concept. If you are a person who requires proof, you will probably not find it here. However, if you accept Aristotle's thoughts on influence (Rapp 2010), you may feel that there is merit in borrowing concepts that are aligned with OrgZoo.

BECOMING ADAPTABLE

OrgZoo is a hybrid cocreated from aspects of many disciplines and approaches. Each of these techniques has a deep body of literature that is easily accessible in an internet search. Use these lists as a starting-point for your own explorations.

Primary influences

Metaphor, symbolism and life

Metaphor is a powerful way to distil complex concepts into simplified communication mechanisms. A metaphor can help people to understand something that is more complex. It is not the literal thing, but something familiar that the person can relate to. Describing a behaviour can be subjective and complex; using a metaphor to represent that behaviour is more easily understood and simpler to convey.

Metaphor is embedded into every culture and language in many ways. Language itself is a metaphor, in that a word represents the thing it describes but is not the thing itself. We do not have the time to fully describe everything we deal with every day from first principles, so we create words to represent those things.

Metaphors are symbolic representations of the things we engage with every day. They enable us to simplify the way we communicate and be creative about the important, and mundane, aspects of our lives. A statement like "they are a pig" clearly refers to the undesirable aspects of that person, probably that they are messy or greedy in their behaviour. As we go through life's journey (a metaphor in itself), we use metaphor every day without even knowing it. It is a natural part of how we interact and communicate with others.

This natural relationship with metaphor makes OrgZoo a perfect choice as the basis for personal and professional

10. Theories embedded into OrgZoo philosophies

development. Participants can immediately engage in interactions because the OrgZoo metaphors seem familiar. They do not need to learn a new language or technique: they simply play in a way that symbolises their life experiences.

Action learning, andragogy and flipped-classroom learning approaches

Action learning, or learning by doing, is a well-defined academic approach. There is a huge body of literature on experiential learning, action learning, and action research. These are deliberately designed into the way OrgZoo interactions and games operate, because they work well.

Andragogy is an academic term relating to adult learning. It is an open facilitation approach that stimulates interactions between people to share insights from their own experiences as part of the learning to create new possibilities. This is distinct from traditional content-based learning, or pedagogy (although a general term for traditional learning, pedagogy is derived from 'child learning'). In OrgZoo interactions there is no content. The interactions are all learner-centred and cocreative, drawing on the experiences of the paticipants.

Flipped classroom is the method in which learners read about the concepts and content first, then come to a formal interaction like a classroom or workshop, either face to face or virtual. Participants familiarise themselves with the concepts in advance, so the time spent together is focused on asking questions and interacting around the concepts based on their collective life experiences. The core of the learning happens in the social interactions and through the questions asked of the facilitator and each other. This concept is deeply embedded into all OrgZoo interactions.

BECOMING ADAPTABLE

Creativity, cocreation and collaboration

The future is more about what we collaborate to cocreate than it is about what we already know. Yet many teaching approaches focus on knowing existing facts (which may or may not remain valid in the future). Whilst learning from existing knowledge is important, especially learning from our mistakes, it is not the best way to prepare for the future.

We create the future through collaborating with others to cocreate new insights and innovations. This is amplified through action learning and facilitated conversations that enable shifts in mindset and behaviour. Effective collaboration builds capabilities that enable us to be stronger competitors. Collaboration and competition are not opposing approaches: they are strategic partners in sustained success.

Followership, management and leadership

It's a common misconception that there is a linear path from being a capable person to becoming a manager, then to becoming a leader. These are three separate aspects of being human. Understanding the relationships between Knowing, Doing and Being (Shelley 2017) and how these relate to following, managing and leading, is important to *Becoming Adaptable*.

Over time there have been a plethora of models for leadership and management, each with their own strengths and weaknesses. Throughout our lives there are moments in which all three are appropriate and moments in which they are inappropriate. They are vastly different mindsets, which benefit from conscious choice.

— Followership (accepting the advice of others who are

10. Theories embedded into OrgZoo philosophies

> more capable of making decisions in that context) is appropriate when we are in unfamiliar territory.

— Management is a convergent focus on resolving a problem, mostly using existing knowledge and capabilities. It is short-term and present-focused.

— Leadership is divergent and future-focused, looking to create new insights and possibilities.

The behaviours that align with each are different. It is not about right and wrong, or your developmental stage: it is how your behaviour, mindset and actions are aligned to your context and purpose. Understanding when to lead, when to follow, and when to manage, is a critical element of personal and professional success. These types of questions are considered in the design phase of OrgZoo interactions.

Reflective practice

Reflection is the most important part of learning. Traditionally it is the process through which one thinks about the implications and alternatives of something, either after it happened or as it is happening. These important actions were named 'reflection on action' and 'reflection in action' by Donald Schˆn (1983).

In OrgZoo design, 'reflect on future actions' (Shelley 2012) is added as a prompt to consider possible behavioural states that may be desired. In the OrgZoo activities it is common to assess the optimal behaviour for situations that have not yet happened. This helps guide participants on how to choose their behaviour more effectively when the moment comes. This forward-looking perspective allows us to influence future states and cultures.

BECOMING ADAPTABLE

Language and communication

Language is the tool through which people (and machines) communicate meaning and influence. It has many forms including verbal, body, gesture, tone, dialect and process.

Language is a highly complex entity that greatly affects how we come to understand what another person or intelligence means. Without language we struggle to understand each other or convey intent widely.

With this complexity comes the opportunity to misread the meaning. Language can be an effective way to inform or mislead others, especially when combining senses of verbal, fluidity, tone and body language elements.

Comprehensive learning, beyond a transfer of existing knowledge, relies on the complete communication cycle:

— an initial transmission of a concept

— receipt and reflection to interpret and understand the meaning and intent of the sending party

— feedback from the receiver to confirm comprehensive understanding

— confirmation or correction by the original provider

In much communication this sequence of activities gets confused or, worse, deliberately misrepresented. When this happens, the communication changes the meaning of the message and therefore its impact.

Understanding the relationship between language, communication, and understanding is an important part of facilitating conversations. OrgZoo interactions are specifically designed to transfer the intent or generate the desired learning outcomes. Sometimes an experience of being (safely) misled

10. Theories embedded into OrgZoo philosophies

can highlight potential blind spots like subconscious bias. Recognising these weaknesses in one's capabilities is an important part of *Becoming Adaptable*. When facilitating OrgZoo activities (or anything), one must be aware of the importance of all steps in the process and seek to confirm they have all been done effectively. This can be assessed by watching, or more formally by asking the participants to demonstrate their ability to act on the intent of the messaging or learning.

Visualisation

Visualisation is the art and science of presenting concepts, meaning or insights in a graphical form to convey an idea or assist with interpretation. This could be a physical format such as artwork, statistical charts, maps, photography, video; or it can be a less tangible creative medium such as interpretive dance. In its most esoteric form, a visualisation can occur solely in your mind, perhaps stimulated by deep thought or reflective conversation.

Creative visualisations are becoming easier to generate because of the power of graphical algorithms. Images of OrgZoo characters were deliberately designed as cartoons to embed an element of visual humour into the interactions.

Visualisation is discussed in more detail later in this chapter.

Humour

Edward de Bono has been quoted as saying that humour is the most under-utilised management tool.

Employed well and appropriately, humour can achieve great outcomes. It can de-stress situations and encourage people to

BECOMING ADAPTABLE

participate. Humour is often used in OrgZoo activities as a conversation starter or to stimulate a positive mindset.

If humour is not used in a caring and inclusive manner, there is a risk of offending people. Always ensure that humour is carefully considered before being applied (although this can reduce the spontaneity somewhat).

Philosophy and social constructivism

Not everyone deeply reflects on their philosophy of life. It manifests itself in what we believe. Some people quite happily float through life reacting to what happens, either enthusiastically or in a dramatic negative way, or anything in between.

Exploring your own philosophy can be a deeply moving and informing activity to undertake. It takes time to consider why you are who you are and what actions make you happy or sad and why. Some people subscribe to fate — a deterministic view that whatever was meant to happen will happen, generally outside the individual's influence.

I believe it is possible to change the future through one's actions and behaviours. My philosophy is formed around acting to create social value and helping others to do this too. This requires a belief that we have the capability and capacity to influence what happens next (although admittedly we do not always have the opportunity or resources to implement our preferred actions).

The concept of social constructivism suggests that knowledge, understanding and meaning are generated by people interacting to share ideas and create insights together. That is, new concepts and possibilities are the outcomes of social interactions. We can cocreate new insights from how we

10. Theories embedded into OrgZoo philosophies

interact with each other. Combining these two suggests that we can achieve new opportunities together.

Conversation structure

Conversation structure is described in several places in this book (see for example Chapter 6). It is the central tool of OrgZoo interactions and used in a range of formats.

Gamification

Games work because they draw people into the activities and maintain their interest. In recent years there has been a significant increase in the availability and use of games for professional and personal development (Allen and Sutton 2019). OrgZoo has involved games since before the original book was published in 2007.

Complexity science and emergence

Understanding the differences between chaotic, complex, complicated, and simple situations is necessary for a facilitator. The best place to start on this is David Snowden's work on the Cynefin Framework (Snowden and Boone 2007). More recent articles and videos are available on the internet discussing this important knowledge and how it has continued to evolve with experiences and application.

Emergence is an area of knowledge that is separate from, but related to, complexity science. Emergence, as the word suggests, is allowing ideas and concepts to rise out of the interaction and influence the outcomes. For example, ideas and insights emerge through discussions. Participants' confidence emerges from practice, reflection and feedback. Recognising the role of emergence is important to the creative

BECOMING ADAPTABLE

aspects of social exchanges. Social cocreation accelerates when we actively support an environment that stimulates and recognises emergence.

OrgZoo facilitations are not aligned to one or the other of these models. Rather, the activities incorporate multiple components to varying degrees. The challenge for facilitators is to know in the moment when to draw on one or the other model — or a combination — to sustain the flow of the interactions. Becoming Adaptable benefits from deep familiarity with the concepts and confidence with to apply them in action as required. See Chapter 7 for practical examples, and the Appendix for a wider set of elements that influence the success of facilitation.

Secondary influences

Less obviously than the primary influences, OrgZoo and *Becoming Adaptable* draw in ideas from a range of other professional and academic disciplines.

- Learning theories (various)
- Emotional intelligence
- Design thinking
- Diversity
- Systems thinking
- Critical thinking
- Strategic thinking
- Human-centred design
- Psychology and psychometrics
- Knowledge management
- Capability development

10. Theories embedded into OrgZoo philosophies

> Problem-based learning
> Body language and reading people
> Project management

This list of elements can be easily searched on the internet to gain a deeper understanding. Although these secondary influences may not be included in every OrgZoo activity, they are used in some dialogue aspects and in how outcomes are captured. Deep experience of all these disciplines is not necessary, though it is certainly helpful to maintain confidence and levels of participation among participants. The Appendix lists resources for some of these influences.

The power of visualisation for creative cocreation

Visualisation is mentioned throughout this book because it is an extremely important part of sensemaking. People make sense of something by visualising it in their mind, or in their imagination if it is yet to become real. Visual representations have always been an important part of how humans express their thoughts and feelings, from the days of cave paintings through all eras of human development.

In recent years, visualisation techniques have exploded because of computing power and advanced algorithms. This is driven by a desire to understand complex data and find ways to represent the patterns of insights that can be drawn from it. Big data collection and analysis in real time enable evidence-based decisions as information emerges. Visualisations such as network analyses explicitly represent the connections between complex sets of data that previously would have taken significant time to percolate through manual analysis.

The relevance of visualisation to OrgZoo lies in several aspects. Representing behaviour as a recognisable OrgZoo character helps

BECOMING ADAPTABLE

workshop participants to literally see the behaviours and communicate this with others. The arrangement of OrgZoo cards on the table is a visualisation of a culture: the patterns of behaviour that are accepted and rejected by that social group. The Behavioural DNA images are a way to see the overall diversity of perspectives in a group of people. Such insights are difficult to describe in words. Visualisations like these are quick to cocreate and extremely valuable as conversation starters.

One of my most-used visualisations is shown in Figure 10.3. It highlights the complexity of behavioural matches and mismatches. Exploring the complex interactions between people with different behavioural expectations is challenging. This visualisation enables people to see and discuss why behavioural misunderstandings happen. It also reinforces why our chosen behaviours can lead to constructive outcomes or destructive conflict.

This visualisation enables comparison of the behavioural profiles of different entities (people, teams, or organisations).

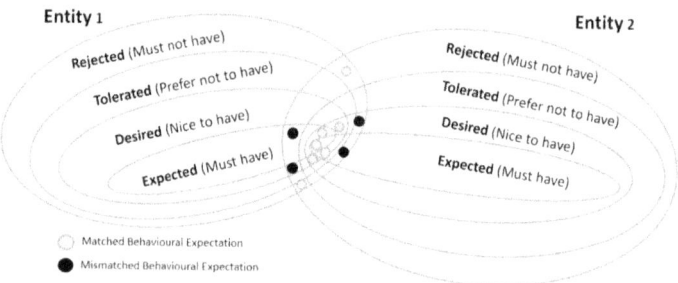

Figure 10.3 Comparing behavioural patterns across cultures: culture clash or creativity?

Using OrgZoo character cards, we can layer the behavioural expectations:

— Behaviours the entity absolutely expects is at the centre. These are the must-haves, the core of the culture.

10. Theories embedded into OrgZoo philosophies

— Around that core we place the desired behaviours. These are the nice-to-haves that make a positive contribution but are not absolutely essential.

— We then cross over into the tolerated behaviours. These are behaviours that the entity prefers not to have. We can observe them without going into conflict, but we would prefer if they did not happen.

— In the final outer layer are the behaviours we reject. These are the must-not-haves.

This arrangement of behaviours is the foundation of Behavioural DNA analysis. It is useful to compare the profiles of two entities and see where matches and mismatches happen.

The matches are where the same behaviour falls in the same layer for each entity (indicated by grey dots in Figure 10.3). These are the basis of connection and a sense of belonging.

Where one entity expects a behaviour and another rejects it, the natural reaction is conflict (indicated by black dots in Figure 10.3). However, with better adaptability and open mindsets, conflict does not need to be inevitable. We can create an opening for deeper understanding by widening the tolerance layer and narrowing the rejection layer of each culture. Along with constructive conversations, this creates new possibilities and reduces conflict.

Facilitating conversations that enable the differences to be constructively explored, we can create the potential for learning. Engaging in creative friction around differences (in behaviour or ideas) can open mindsets to different ways of interacting and, in turn, drive cultural development and innovation.

Ethical facilitation

There is a spectrum of roles around conversation and interactions. It starts at complete control over what can be said and done (dictatorship) through to totally open dialogue (no control and

BECOMING ADAPTABLE

mostly no result). There is a sliding scale of balance, mixing control and openness to contribution, across a range of the roles played. For example, an advocate is not as strong as a dictator but exercises some control and avoids complete openness.

A good facilitator should be neutral. Their role is to engage people in a conversation that develops emergent ideas from the participants. The facilitator mostly asks challenging questions to get the participants to reflect deeply about aspects of the topic. The faciliator is a role model, maintaining their own professional and ethical manner and ensuring that others do as well.

Some facilitators attempt to influence participants towards agreeing with a particular perspective, or add their own personal insights to the conversation. Ethical facilitation requires that all parties involved in an activity clearly understand the role they play. Stating that you are playing one role, while in fact advocating a hidden agenda, is unethical.

SUCCESS STORY
Thai business scale-up

Genevieve Lim
OZAN Practitioner, Thailand

Context (where and when)

This case was facilitated for a small wellness company that provides intelligent computerised training equipment and evidence-based exercising concepts for senior exercise, rehabilitation and wellness. The CEO has a vision to establish the organisation as an innovative company and to develop a dynamic team to become the market lead in Thailand and neighbouring countries. The company faces many challenges to achieve this desired outcome, including operational management, staff capacity, knowledge management, delivery of business strategies and above all the prevailing outbreak of COVID-19.

Why?

To assess the existing business practices, a series of conversations was conducted with the CEO and staff on its master plan for 2021 and 2022, product knowledge, and service concepts. Co-assessment of sales performance and social media impacts were carried out to identify weaknesses. Individually, the staff completed OrgZoo activities to identify their roles in the organisation. The objective was to involve and engage the CEO and staff to have common understanding of the behaviours and relationships that would enable cocreation of innovative business strategies for the next two years.

Who?

The company has ten team members who are responsible for product, marketing, sales and service. It focuses on government projects considering the high prices of the imported equipment from Finland and the larger scale of the projects. Having an

BECOMING ADAPTABLE

innovative image is critical for the success of the business. As such, the company recruited two consultants to transform the company to be innovative with high level of adaptability and dynamism.

What?

A series of workshops over a 5-week period was implemented to develop creative and innovative mindsets among staff. Using design thinking, the staff began to initiate and work on new ideas for achievable outcomes. A 6-month weekly training program began as the next stage towards the transformation. Learning took place to build the capacity of the staff to design and implement new strategies. The OrgZoo Ambassador engaged the staff in activities to explore behavioural change to be ready for disruption in the business. Focusing on senior customers' journeys stimulated behavioural change. The staff became proactive as they engaged in the activities.

How? (did OrgZoo activities help)

Timely interaction with the coach helped staff members to realise the inefficiency of their instruction-oriented practice. OrgZoo activities strengthened the responses to and preparedness for cultural change. Revealing the master plan enhanced information flow and allowed staff to see the urgency for change. The new sets of behavioural DNA significantly fostered the need to adapt and build dynamic capabilities.

Outputs (tangible short-term value delivered)

The formation of a new Behavioural DNA of the company to push the strategic plans of the firm.

Development of corporate business plan and integration of new projects of the four teams in the same direction.

Effective learning programs to support the strategic plan to establish first flagship store by 2022.

Outcome (intangible long-term value delivered)

The CEO became more open and listen to support his teams well.

The staff working attitude has significantly improved. They now collaborate to deliver workable plans.

The company saw the value of being a learning organisation and a knowledge organisation, as they evolved into an innovative firm.

BECOMING ADAPTABLE

11. MindFLEX — the complexity of parallel perspective facilitation

One challenging aspect of facilitation is maintaining multiple interdependent perspectives in your mind at same time as being aware of what others may be thinking. The basic idea of this was introduced in my book *KNOWledge SUCCESSion* (Shelley 2017) and is further developed here.

I refer to this state of being as mindFLEX, to highlight the differences from, and limitations of, mindSET.

Although not a completely correct perspective, the SET at the end of mindset suggests a particular solid state. Carol Dweck (2008) talked about two types of mindset, fixed and growth. For many people, this is not a this-or-that dichotomy. It is more of sliding scale. For some aspects of life, one can be quite of fixed mind, whereas for other aspects one may have an open mind (a growth mindset). Where a person is on the scale of completely fixed to completely open, in any moment their response depends on how familiar, and therefore how confident, they are with the situation they are in. People can be flexible of mind, shifting across the scale

BECOMING ADAPTABLE

in moments of time: being certain about something can quickly change when a new idea or perspective is unexpectedly introduced.

MindFLEX is a superior, harmonious state of being. It involves synchronously considering many perspectives (emotional, intellectual, spiritual, behavioural and social, for example) on a situation in the past, present or possible future. Being in this multiple state of mind elevates the senses and connections being made between people and concepts. This stimulates collaboration and cocreation in interactions with participants in the activities.

Figure 11.1 shows the various aspects being held in active parallel thinking and feeling as the interactions occur. Having all these in parallel active play in the mind enables you to see situations from multiple perspectives and provides a richer set of views on how to interpret and act upon options.

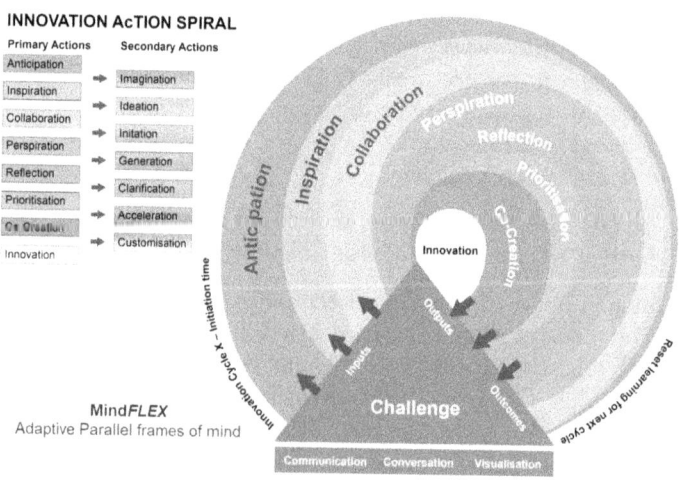

Figure 11.1 MindFLEX is the ability to hold multiple perspectives in mind in parallel

11. MindFLEX parallel perspective facilitation

A mindFLEX cycle varies in the proportion of each aspect at different stages. There is no special formula, as the dynamics emerge through team interactions. The key is to keep all in play throughout the cycle. This ensures the team are not tempted to fall back into serial activities, as that will limit the synergies generated by the mindFLEX activity.

MindFLEX elevates our individual and collective awareness that our own perspective is limited because it is only informed by our own interpretations and experiences. Once we understand that it is possible to see things from a range of perspectives, and add to that a range of perspectives from others, we can greatly increase the insights we have before engaging in decisions and actions. In effect we can engage in a collective state that adapts across a scale of perspectives to more deeply understand the situations we face.

For the facilitator demonstrating mindFLEX, their ability to be openly collaborating with one participant and simultaneously reigning in another in a professional manner is a learned skill. MindFLEX leverages reflective practice in the present, informed by the past, to generate desired future outcomes. It is guided from multiple positions of the people involved in the activity to cocreate new insights, knowledge and outcomes.

Ideally, when reflecting on your own deliberations and opportunities, the initial reflection is aimed at achieving future desired outcomes, acted on in the present, whilst informed by past experiences. Reflecting before, during and after an event are all useful investments to generate optimal outcomes. Add to that reflecting from a range of functional perspectives: social, cultural, ethical, intellectual, commercial, political, environmental, technical et cetera.

Once you have gathered some perspectives of your own, you can gather feedback from others, either through asking them what they think without prompts or by stating your thoughts and asking them for feedback. However, when facilitating, your own thoughts are

BECOMING ADAPTABLE

not as relevant. You want the participants to go through this process without them being heavily influenced by your own personal views.

Although this multifaceted reflection and feedback process can be time-consuming, it is effective and generates better outcomes. Too often people focus on getting a quick answer at the expense of the quality of the answer. The world focuses too much on efficiency (speed) at the expense of effectiveness (quality in context). With a little more time investment, it is possible to achieve more.

Complex situations are not best addressed by converging on the challenges as this-or-that alternatives. They are better served when discussed in open dialogue with an open and curious mind asking "This *and* that, *and* those *and* which others?" before prioritising. This divergent Agile approach can be thought of as mindFLEX rather than mindset.

SUCCESS STORY
Applying OrgZoo to shift mindsets

Frank Connolly
OrgZoo Ambassador, Australia

Context (where and when)

I have applied the OrgZoo techniques across industries for many years. I find applying the associated metaphors and behaviours provides an elegantly simple and safe way of drawing responses and alternative perspectives that may not have otherwise surfaced. 'Elephants in the room' (hidden issues) are very difficult to tackle when they sit silently rather than being shared in open conversation. However, when we take them and place them on a card or wall, it becomes open season. The OrgZoo methods allow participants to self-reflect upon their own behaviours in a safe and fun way. This in turn enables greatly improved design and outcomes going forward.

Why?

Except in limited circumstances, you just cannot tell anyone anything. Too many change initiatives are based upon telling and demonstrating a better way forward. Not enough involve cocreation and self-reflection on the current state. The OrgZoo metaphors are a great way to aid participants in considering current behaviours and practices, and then internally acknowledge where the most effective change might be applied. If it is invented within, and not imposed from without, it has a far greater likelihood of sticking. The Org Zoo encourages invention from within and stimulates people to open their minds towards alternative possibilities. The inclusive conversations lead to mindset shift, both individually and collectively.

BECOMING ADAPTABLE

Who?

I was involved in experimenting with some of Arthur's early ideas soon after the book was being written. The initial activities were even before the character cards were released. In my role as the lead of a large government knowledge exchange network, I coordinated many professional development sessions to build capabilities and relationships, within and across government agencies. People involved in the workshops (facilitated by a range of consultants and learning facilitators) were for all levels and disciplines of government and ranged from small groups though to hundreds, depending in the event. Later, in my own independent practice, I continued to use OrgZoo activities to stimulate conversations about important topics that were otherwise challenging to engage people around.

What?

A variety of workshops have been facilitated over a period of several years for different purposes. OrgZoo techniques were often combined with other tools for innovation and creativity to amplify the learning. Sometimes the OrgZoo activity was used as an ice breaker, and other times as a deeper approach to explore a more complex issue, such as behavioural challenges in a team.

How? (did OrgZoo activities help)

One of the most powerful benefits of OrgZoo is its ability to get the teams involved in conversations outside their normal patterns of behaviour. It is only by experiencing this alternative way to interact, that they realise just how limiting their own mindsets can be. As a case in point, we had one large government client that took five phone conversations with different managers before we were engaged to complete some innovation related training. In each conversation, each manager went to great pains to point out that they were already an innovative and highly collaborative organisation that operated at best practice. The first exercise we put them thorough was the Invisible Maze. Upon conclusion, all fifty people present were questioning their capabilities to effectively collaborate in teams and as an organisation. This realisation was entirely through their own reflection in conversation afterwards. As this realisation was their own collective insight, it carried a great deal more weight than being informed of the same by any consultant!

Outputs (tangible short-term value delivered)

Behavioural profiles for the teams involved highlighting stimulants and barriers for change.

Actions to be taken to engage people in constructive change and less resistance to that change.

Lists of cocreated ideas to apply and continue communications in future activities.

Outcomes (intangible long-term value delivered)

People enjoy the creative engagement that OrgZoo provides and the conversations it stimulates. In my experience they learn more and build relationships better and they last back in the workplace when they use these inclusive approaches. Part of the benefits of this is the shift towards a more open mind and greater awareness that challenges are better discussed than kept hidden. To use another unrelated animal metaphor: the horse will always enjoy drinking more if it goes to the water itself. OrgZoo methods are a great way of leaving the stable door open for this to occur.

BECOMING ADAPTABLE

Part D

Start becoming adaptable for YOU

BECOMING ADAPTABLE

12. Behaviour can be an asset or a liability

Behaviour influences social connections in both directions

The way we interact with each other determines the type of relationships we form, maintain and destroy. We have stronger connections to those we align with on aspects like expectations, perceptions and culture. Relationships with connecting expectations build over time if this alignment continues. However, if our expectations shift as a result of experiences or change of circumstances, so do our behaviours. These changes can strengthen relationships, if we are actively interacting with other parties and adapting together. If the shift is different for different parties, the relationship can be suddenly disrupted, or wane over time as the connections fade.

This is often most evident when you see someone you have not seen for a long time. They are quite different from how you remember them. Every experience changes us somewhat, and a collection of small shifts over time adds up to a more noticeable change. The

BECOMING ADAPTABLE

more regularly you interact and share your ideas, dreams and insights with another person, the closer you grow together. However, once you stop conversing and asking each other for their thoughts, the more you grow apart. This results in the two parties becoming less connected, which in turn shifts the behaviours you (mostly subconsciously) display towards the other person. Such relationships can fall into a pattern — like visiting relatives only at defined occasions, without maintaining a deeper ongoing relationship. Alternatively, and more commonly, the relationship slowly decays and the person drifts away from your inner circle of friends.

Relationships, like all important assets, need to be maintained to preserve and build the value they bring to all parties in them. Without mutual value being exchanged, they deteriorate. Without regular conversations and interaction, they easily become misaligned. How we behave with each other is a significant factor in our relationships and this is why it is important to match our behaviours well.

Behaviour is contextual and neither right nor wrong in an absolute sense. All the OrgZoo character behaviours have a niche in which they are aligned with the situation (helpful to relationship building). Equally, there are situations in which these same behaviours are misaligned with the situation (damaging social interactions). Table 12.1 lists examples of situations when each of the OrgZoo characters is matched (helpful) and misaligned (unhelpful). Conscious choice of behaviour is linked to the context in which you are interacting. The situation can change in a moment — with one comment or action, or some external influence like an unpredicted emergency.

The examples provided as matched (helpful) and mismatched (unhelpful) in Table 12.1 look similar, but have almost the opposite impact. This is because the behaviour being displayed is the same, but the situation is different and so the outcome of the behaviour is also different. This is where capabilities like sensemaking, emotional

12. Behaviour can be an asset or a liability

intelligence, empathy and critical thinking enable better judgements as to which behaviour is best matched to the situation. Making informed decisions about your behaviour in the context is essential to enable the optimal outcomes.

Table 12.1 Examples of Situations with Matched and Mismatched Behaviours for each OrgZoo Character

OrgZoo character	Matched behaviour: context in which helpful	Mismatched behaviour: context in which not helpful
Ant	Getting things done when strong task orientation is required.	Focus on task completion when creativity and alternative thinking required
Bee	Inclusive interactions and communication in collaborative team activities.	Aggressively defending the team despite them doing unhelpful activities
Chameleon	Fitting into the current status quo to go with the flow	Not challenging others when alternative options are better.
Dog	Supportive of the team with absolute loyalty	Blindly following leadership into a crisis without critical thinking
Eagle	Inspiring others as a role model for decisive action	Acting too swiftly when a considered decision may have been more constructive
Feline	Ensuring productivity among team members	Playing mind games to reinforce their own position in the hierarchy

BECOMING ADAPTABLE

OrgZoo character	Matched behaviour: context in which helpful	Mismatched behaviour: context in which not helpful
Gibbon	Leveraging humour to reduce tensions	Not focusing on the key issues in a crisis
Hyena	Networking with colleagues to ambush challenges through shared insights and resources	Politicking to call on return favours that may compromise others
Insect beneficial	Providing insights and experiences to accelerate resolutions	Advocating for a particular option when a range of alternatives may work
Insect pestiferous	Provide a variety of ideas from external sources	Self-interested actions being advocated which may not be best options
Jackal	Social care and emotional support for the group members	Taking advantage of privileged position, often leveraging deferred power
Kid	New creative (naïve) insights that stimulate creativity and innovation	Offering naïve ideas that cause distractions for resolving a crisis
Lion	Controlling processes and resources to ensure safety and productivity	Leveraging position to force others to follow directives against their will
Mouse	Engaging in productive work when focused and well managed	Engaging in non-productive or even destructive activities when bored

12. Behaviour can be an asset or a liability

OrgZoo character	Matched behaviour: context in which helpful	Mismatched behaviour: context in which not helpful
Nematode	Indulging oneself to relax when on holidays, so you return to work completely recharged and ready	Almost any work situation — taking benefit without giving back is unforgivable and bound to destroy relationships and damage culture
Owl	Mentoring others to become adaptable and knowledgeable	Rarely, perhaps being too open and not pushing for mentees to act more quickly in important developmental needs
Piranha	Aggressively tearing a problem apart to remove the issue	Engaging in damaging gossip to undermine people
Quercus robur	Philanthropy and giving are almost always beneficial when well directed towards deserving recipients	Rarely, perhaps if too soft on some who may be taking benefit, but not fully deserving of the support
Rattlesnake	Highlighting they are challenged by your presence by making a lot of noise about an issue (without striking)	Making a lot of noise about minor challenges
Sloth	Waiting to allow things to settle for themselves, rather than blowing them up into big issues	Not acting fast enough to correct situations before they become a bigger issue

BECOMING ADAPTABLE

OrgZoo character	Matched behaviour: context in which helpful	Mismatched behaviour: context in which not helpful
Triceratops	Stubbornly refusing the change things that should be maintained as is for good reason	Stubbornly refusing to change to better approaches and good evidence to support the benefits
Unicorn	Creatively offering very different options without restraint	Offering alternative ideas that are totally disconnected from reality of the moment that are simply impractical
Vulture	Finding weaknesses in the plan or system and taking out the weaker options before they become an issue	Criticising problems after they have happened (when perhaps they could have highlighted the risks earlier, in time for preventable actions)
Whale	Bring intellectual insights to the conversations, especially around specialist areas like technology, knowledge and science	Sometimes too smart for their own good and beach themselves because of their certainty of being right
X-Breed	Provide a range of perspectives into the conversation based on prior experiences and learning and recommend which they believe is best and why	Overconfidence based on their multitalented capabilities and knowledge can lead them to make a limited decision that does not consider wider or longer-term implications

12. Behaviour can be an asset or a liability

OrgZoo character	Matched behaviour: context in which helpful	Mismatched behaviour: context in which not helpful
Yak	Some of the greatest inventions come from errors, for example penicillin. Enthusiasm to act and see what happens can generate new insights	Actions without appropriate reflection can cause a lot of unpredicted collateral damage, both in short term and longer term
Snail Hidden background behaviours*	Getting in to do the basic routine activities in background, without the need to be noticed or provided with kudos	Background routines can become quite outdated and inefficient without regular review. Limited attention to such activities can become poor habit

For a more detailed description of Snail characteristics, see the original OrgZoo book glossary.

Consciously choosing and reflecting on your behaviour for greater impact

Understanding why, how and when behaviour can be an asset or a liability helps us to play out the challenges of life. Our reputation, the trust we generate, and the relationships we build or destroy, are outcomes of the cumulative decisions we make. Have you become a trusted and inspirational leader of others, or do people shy away from you? Are you both a follower of other inspirational leaders and an authentic leader to your own followers? Do you listen to others and collaborate with them to generate social value, or do you seek to extract value from the system for self-benefit?

BECOMING ADAPTABLE

I have previously defined leadership as having willing, intelligent followers. *Willing* because leading by force is unsustainable. True leadership inspires others to follow because they want to. *Intelligent*, because you don't want people to just follow you blindly. You want them to consider why you are worthy of their loyalty, trust and respect, and to consciously decide you are a person of credibility and high ethical standards who will make a positive difference.

The opposite of the above is also true. Many evil leaders have existed throughout history with considerable success and support (although not generally sustained in the long term). A set of behaviours totally unacceptable to some can be attractive to others. This is particularly evident with people demonstrating the OrgZoo characters such as Lion (control and command, seen by supporters as strength) and Rattlesnake (political manoeuvring, seen by supporters as smart). These same behaviours are seen by opponents as controlling, manipulative and unethical. Our interpretations of behaviour are biased by our own position and stance on the person and the situation. This is where deeper reflection and reading the perspectives of opponents can be very helpful, as it highlights insights that you will not see yourself.

Becoming Adaptable means challenging your own values, behaviours and actions on a regular basis, and supporting this challenge with evidence whenever you can. This enables you to strengthen your belief in your own decisions and more robustly argue why they are the right fit for yourself and the people you serve and care about. Too many people just read what they already believe into a situation and reject other perspectives without deeper consideration. Narrow acceptance of 'truths' is a dangerous strategy that limits behavioural adaptability. You do not need to accept all others' perspectives, or challenge your values on every new possibility. However, it is helpful to have a deeper understanding of what motivates other people and why they hold their beliefs.

In short, it is beneficial to understand and choose your own behaviour wisely and in a way that is aligned with your desired outcomes. Do

12. Behaviour can be an asset or a liability

this authentically and transparently and you will positively influence others, without the need to manipulate them.

Understanding others' behaviour for greater influence

It is rare to face absolutely clear alternatives such as a single perfect (or disastrous) outcome. Many decisions in life are not absolutely right or wrong and the situation is often not clear. For example, think about being on a first date. You are mostly exploring the other person's preferences and assessing how they match your expectations. So the behavioural dance is not pre-set choreography, but a divergent and emergent exploration to assess matches and mismatches (often with a few toes being stepped on along the way). Often is it only afterwards that we learn how well or poorly we assessed the signals and whether we reacted to them in a way that was appreciated by the other person.

Sometimes in a workplace there are not good and bad options, only poor and worse! How do you decide which is the least damaging action overall? Anyone can easily make good decisions between right and wrong, or good and bad. Your real mettle as a leader and as a person is demonstrated when you have to make those tough decisions between terrible and disastrous; and by how you behave when explaining your decision and actions to others.

How others judge you determines what level of influence you have on them. Ideally, this is a conscious reflection and proactive decision, although it is often subconsciously and reactive. I sometimes ask people why they like/support or dislike/reject a certain leader or person. The answers are often quite shallow, especially if you dig in and search for the evidence that supports that opinion. Sometimes political correctness jumps in as a defence mechanism. For example, you may get a diversion tactic such as "You can't ask me that," or sometimes a more aggressive (actually

BECOMING ADAPTABLE

defensive) retort like "Are you trying judge me?" implying that judgement is inherently a bad thing.

We all make judgements. They are important elements of success and relationships. In fact, if we don't make judgements, and just engage without informed reflections, we are easily misguided. Without well considered judgements, we may end up mixing with inappropriate people and making compromised decisions. Deciding who to mix with and who to avoid is a critical judgement. The outcome of that judgement is evaluated by others you interact with. Judgement is necessary — but biased and ill-informed judgements are dangerous; that is, making decisions that lack evidence (which is usually more subjective than objective in social contexts) or are not based on ethical considerations.

People who make good judgements and act ethically are generally respected, even if they are from an opposing political stance or culture. You can respect the decisions of someone who chooses differently from you — if you can see why they make those choices in their particular context.

I often play a developmental game called "The Human Spectrum" in my workshops. I ask a question that prompts a spectrum of responses and the participants arrange themselves along a line to represent where they stand on that question. Typically the spectrum runs from 'absolutely agree' to 'absolutely disagree,' with any position in between. We then engage in *Conversations That Matter* about why each person chose their position along the line. Many interpretations of the question arise; some people change their response, while others become more steadfast in their original choice.

Then, to demonstrate how perspectives can change with context, I give the same question a different context. Again, a certain number of participants will change their responses in reaction to this new perspective. Watching people move along the line is a powerful visualisation of influences, choices and differences. (This exercise also works well in an online environment.)

12. Behaviour can be an asset or a liability

The point of the activity is not to say who is right and who is wrong. It is about exploring why individuals take their own perspective on any given situation, and when and how they might adjust that stance.

We all influence other people, even by not acting or participating. How we influence — to attract or repel others — is heavily determined by our behaviour. You can allow this to happen naturally (that is, subconsciously) or you can deliberately plan your behaviour to achieve better outcomes.

Consciously managing your behaviour is possible most of the time, with practice and feedback. It is not a bad thing, as long as you are true to your values and acting ethically. Done this way, you positively influence others.

Compromising your own values and ethics for personal gain at the expense of others is not a good approach and is considered manipulative (although not uncommon). Manipulation is commonly understood as a form of influence. It moves people to behave differently, but for compromised or misguided reasons. Manipulation is perceived as a negative approach that is usually done to gain value from others through unfair or unethical means. Ultimately this approach damages reputation, and for people with a social conscience it can also damage their health and wellbeing (usually once exposed).

Do not get 'who you are' confused with 'what you are'! Who you are is about being true to the fundamental reasons that you feel good about yourself. It is embedded in your values and your positive connections with others in society. It is the foundation of your reputation, spirit and sense of belonging.

What you are is defined in the roles you fill in society and career. It is important to align your roles with who you are, to maintain a balanced wellbeing. If you are being encouraged to compromise who you are to be successful in your role, it is critical for you to reflect deeply on the behaviours you choose to express. Making

BECOMING ADAPTABLE

judgements about how to act and why is best performed as a proactive and reflective activity. Reflecting back on why you made some poor decision usually happens because you have been influenced in a way that compromised your values and you went along without sufficient self-challenge.

In the end, you have to justify your decisions to yourself and those you care about. This is called the grandmother test: if you can't look your grandmother in the eye and honestly explain what you did and why, then you are probably compromising yourself. "I had no choice" is ignored. Trust and reputation are long-term outcomes of good choices over many years. However, trust can be totally destroyed in a moment with a poor decision.

SUCCESS STORY
The University Zoo

Keith De La Rue
OZAN Ambassador, Australia

Context (where and when)

I first became aware of the Organizational Zoo over a decade ago, when I departed from a full-time corporate position to work in consultancy and tertiary education. The richness of the zoo metaphor immediately struck me as an excellent model for understanding the behaviours I had observed in the organisation I had just parted company with.

Why?

I could also see that it would be a powerful tool to use in preparing students for coping with the organisations they would be working in after gaining their qualifications. One complaint I often hear about undergraduate students is that "these kids come into university feeling entitled and wanting to be spoon-fed". What I have observed from working with these students and observing the outcomes from the OrgZoo activities is that this may not be a very fair criticism. My observation is that these students have been pushed for so long through an educational production line that they have not had the time or liberty to be aware of anything outside this narrow experience, let alone to question how to explore beyond it. I have had students talk to me after these classes who have experienced what could only be described as an epiphany.

Who?

Over the last ten years, I have used the Organizational Zoo metaphor and materials in several university courses that I have been engaged in teaching. The subjects have included project management, leadership and business communication in

BECOMING ADAPTABLE

different contexts, in both undergraduate and postgraduate settings. The delivery modes of the material have ranged from remote learning using printed study guides and online discussion for an international audience to face-to-face lectures and interactive workshops at two universities in Melbourne, Australia. In the face-to-face workshops, I have mostly used the Organizational Zoo character cards in group exercises, with additional OrgZoo activities used on many occasions. In each case, I have seen students engage fully with the metaphor.

What?

The activity I have used most frequently is to give one OrgZoo card deck to each student group, and ask them to assemble behaviours that will build an effective team. This usually requires each group to choose a set of five cards to represent each category for expected, desirable, tolerated and rejected behaviours. To achieve the desired results, the group will itself exhibit a range of behaviours. One I often notice is that even though I explicitly direct the students to spread the cards around so that everyone can see them, one student in the group will hold the cards and only pass them on to others when asked to do so. This of course then becomes a talking point on the behaviour being exhibited.

Another similar exercise is to ask students to select cards to represent desired team leadership behaviours. There are always discussions about the place of lion, eagle and owl behaviour in this context, but it is also interesting that most student groups will also select unicorn behaviour as desirable. Students often do not initially understand that the unicorn is the "mythical perfect manager", and further discussion is often necessary for students to recognise that sometimes the inner and outer view of behaviours may not match.

This activity will usually be more readily understood by postgraduate students with some previous workplace experience than by undergraduates, but even many postgraduate students find it an eye-opening experience that helps to explain difficulties they have had dealing with stakeholders in previous workplace environments.

How? (did OrgZoo activities help)

It is always interesting to see how postgraduate students bring real world experiences into these activities. On one occasion, one group included the sloth card in the 'expected' behaviour category. When asked why, they explained that there is always one lazy person in every group, so they decided that it would be more realistic to include it at the outset!

Once students have developed some familiarity with the Organizational Zoo behaviours in the team and leadership context, I will then introduce a set of behaviours that may be exhibited by the team's stakeholders. It is at this point that students become aware of the need for flexibility in behaviours. They come to realise that the behaviours that are conducive to collaborative teamwork (such as Owl, Bee, Quercus robur) will not usually be very effective at dealing with potentially antagonistic stakeholders (such as Lion, Vulture, Chameleon).

Outputs (tangible short-term value delivered)

In every student cohort I have used the Organizational Zoo activities with, many students have provided feedback on the value they have gained from the experience. Once students become familiar with the metaphor, the discussions that follow usually include personal reflections and realisations. For many, it is an extra tool to use to be more effective in their professional lives; for some, it has been a life-changing experience.

Outcomes (intangible long-term value delivered)

Overall, I have found the use of the Organizational Zoo metaphor to be an invaluable element in my teaching. It provides a safe environment for assisting students to understand the power of

BECOMING ADAPTABLE

behaviour, and to help them to understand the importance of taking a conscious, proactive approach to using behaviour to be more effective in whatever professional and personal roles they move into upon graduating.

13. Your journey of becoming

Every personal journey of becoming is unique. We all become something different over time, whether consciously or by simply falling into the sequence of life. Being proactive about what you become, and how you can get there, increases your chances of being happy.

There is a strong sense of accomplishment when you set goals and achieve them over time. It generates positive energy and optimism, and contributes to resilience and wellbeing. Of course, your goals will change over time and that is OK. The foundation of success (however you define it) is to make conscious decisions and nurture a consistent element of improvement over time. When we do this, we lead a more meaningful life.

Knowing how to proactively engage in becoming

The fact that you are reading this book is a good indication that you have already started your journey of becoming. The most powerful word in any endeavour is *start* (closely followed by *persist*). Too

BECOMING ADAPTABLE

often people have a dream they are passionate about, but they never start any actions to bring that dream into reality.

Reading this whole book and engaging in conversations with others about your dreams and how they can be achieved will be very helpful. Engaging on a path with others helps, as the social support generated by travelling together through similar phases makes us stronger and creates synergies. On any day you will be less motivated, but your buddy will be keen and so you persist. Another day, the reverse happens. We always work harder when we know someone else is watching and sharing our feelings and challenges.

Knowing what the journey needs to be is something else. At any point you can think you know what the journey looks like, and that is good. However, the planned journey is not the same as the path taken. This is because we come to know much more as we experience life and its challenges. Our knowledge, capabilities, behavioural range and expectations change as we go through the process of becoming.

Like the images in Chapter 10 we start with one or two perspectives on a few things. As our pathway through life generates more diverse experiences, we can see a range of new possibilities that we could not see before. Alongside this, the world is changing and things occur to create new options that did not exist before. Being proactive about spotting opportunities opens up the scope of choices available. Although we cannot predict as far ahead as we could in a more stable environment, we now get more choices to select from, if we choose an attitude of what I call mindFLEX (see Chapter 11).

Doing activities that generate success

> *"Knowing is not enough; we must apply.*
> *Willing is not enough; we must do."*
>
> — *Johann Wolfgang von Goethe*

13. Your journey of becoming

The great thing about reflection is that we come to a deep understanding of how to attain the best we can, within the constraints we have. However, as Goethe stated several centuries ago, knowing and doing are two different things. *The knowing-doing gap* is a common issue, and the title of an excellent book by Jeffrey Pfeffer and Robert Sutton (1999). Individuals, teams and organisations often fail to do the things they know need to be done. Dreaming, brainstorming, cocreation of new ideas and concepts are wonderful. However, without action these remain in the realm of potential and do not convert into real benefits.

Humans are good at creating plausible excuses for not doing what they know they should. Even the word 'should' itself is an issue. As soon as you hear it, or hear yourself say it, you know the action mentioned is doubtful: I should live a healthier lifestyle; I should talk to my mum more often; I should not make snide remarks; Politicians should not lie; I should work harder when the boss is not around. The list can go on forever. Test yourself and see what happens when you replace *should* with *will*.

The word *should* is deliberately excluded from requirements standards published by the International Standards Organization. Requirements are mandatory actions that must be performed. There is no doubt whether the action is done, or not. This implemented action is judged to comply with an appropriate level of quality, competency and appropriateness to context. Not done means non-compliance. There is no room for *should*.

Your journey of becoming is more complex than a yes or no decision. You should often consider a range of options before you commit. However, once you have made a commitment to a set of actions, replace *should* with *must*. Having committed to a specific action, do it and then commit to an honest self-review of the outcome. Even better, commit to collaborate with a co-learning buddy on your development journey and provide each other with objective, honest feedback. Continue to explore and do more of the things that generate success and less of the things that result in poor outcomes.

BECOMING ADAPTABLE

Little shifts in how we use words make a big difference to how meaning is perceived. In this case, move from inaction to in action! It is far better to decide, act, and learn, than to continue procrastinating.

Becoming a leader and mentor to create your legacy

Some people think it does not matter what happens after you are gone and others believe it is imperative to leave a legacy. I personally believe it is our responsibility to humanity to make a contribution that leaves the world a little better than we found it.

We cannot force others to do what we tell them, but we can be a positive role model who influences others to act in ways that generate mutual benefits. Mentoring is a way of helping someone else achieve their goals. It is about the success of the mentee. The best mentoring is not telling the mentee what to do but asking them challenging questions and sharing alternatives. As a mentor you can offer a range of perspectives and alternative possibilities that opens the mentee's mind. A mentor guides a less experienced person through the challenges they face and enables constructive *Conversations That Matter* for the mentee to more deeply consider where they are going and why. In this way the mentor acts as a tour guide for *Becoming Adaptable*.

Leadership is a complex social relationship that develops over time. It manifests in the capabilities required that enable a person or team to attract "willing intelligent followers" (Shelley 2017). Both adjectives are important. *Willing* is important because an authentic follower wants to follow the leader; that is, they are positively emotionally engaged with the leader's initiatives. You are not a genuine leader if you have to force people to follow you. *Intelligent* is important because it means the follower has actively thought about why they want to follow you. They have critically analysed what you do and why, and have concluded that your purpose and methods align with their values and beliefs. An intelligent follower

13. Your journey of becoming

can see what you are doing is ethical, sustainable and of social benefit.

> *"Every person has the power to make others happy.*
> *Some do it simply by entering a room;*
> *others by leaving the room... Some leave trails of cynicism*
> *and pessimism; others trails of faith and optimism...*
> *What kind of trails do you leave?"*
>
> — *William Arthur Ward*

Perhaps the meaning of life is, as William Ward suggests, to make others happy. The first two lines are both hilarious and deeply sad. His use of paradoxical phrases highlights just how diverse we are and how this shapes the legacy we leave, if there is one at all. The point is not that we are happy about someone's departure and sad about another's: it is that our perspectives are vastly different and that we need to prepare for that by *Becoming Adaptable*. There may not be any absolute truths, but there is a strong sense of reality to the statement that life is neither fair nor equitable. Humans do prefer some people over others. Sometimes the reasons for this are understandable, and sometimes unjust and biased, or just ignorant. A useful self-reflective activity is to ask yourself, what type of person or leader makes you happy and why? Is the answer a deeply considered balance of emotional, social and cognitive aspects, or just a gut feeling?

Acknowledging that not everyone gets the same opportunities or resources to make a positive contribution to the world, you might choose a path that's based on what you can influence. *Becoming Adaptable* will help you to be a leader of others and mentor them to become a contributor more than a consumer.

Of course, your choice is likely to leave an impression on others — either in a good way or otherwise. Your choices determine who and what you become and the legacy you leave.

BECOMING ADAPTABLE

SUCCESS STORY
Life changing behaviour

Mark Boyes
OZAN Ambassador, Australia

Context (where and when)

From an incredibly young age he was recalcitrant; his parents and teachers alike had little influence over his behaviour. In his early years at kinder and school, although not physically aggressive, his unpredictability certainly intimidated many children and adults.

Not getting his own way was the principal challenge for this cheeky and motorised young man. To him life was about having fun, making jokes and being active; being stationary, composed and compliant was not on his agenda. His understanding of the world was hindered by his lack of social, emotional and academic development. At age nine he could only read a few simple words, his handwriting was indecipherable, his speech was slightly impaired and his fine motor skills were deficient. Devastating for all, at age eight his behaviour problems reached crisis point, resulting in emergency hospitalisation.

Why?

Managing change was difficult. His socially destructive behaviours would escalate rapidly when unexpected situations arose. The tantrums surged like a volcanic eruption when he needed to work in groups or play team sports. The root cause of all this unsettled behaviour was a diagnosis of Autism Spectrum Disorder (ASD), Attention Deficit Hyperactivity Disorder (ADHD) and a sprinkling of Oppositional Defiant Disorder (ODD). He was fortunate to have a family that understood the challenges he faced and he became the patient of a leading paediatrician. Nevertheless life was tough and for a long time he bounced from kinder to kinder, then school to school, finally settling into his seventh educational setting late in Grade 3, aged nine.

Who?

The new school environment was nurturing and caring but not without its challenges. Resulting in his expulsion, his previous school had called the police during one of his episodes. An irrational fear of the police ensued, constantly playing on his mind. He saw himself as a 'naughty' boy. His inner auditory loop was filled with negative language which continued to fuel the fire within.

Anxiety compounded all of his concerns. His daily routine included his anguish about seemingly insignificant things. Over time his patterns of behaviour became predicable. There was a clear relationship between certain stressors and social outcomes. His cognitive therapy was focussed on him identifying the triggers and managing appropriate responses. Five sessions of equine therapy were the beginning of his ability to understand the impact of his behaviour on others. Despite this new knowledge, his struggles continued. At school he needed to deal with multiple social interactions, which he found overwhelming. At this time his main goal was to just stay in the classroom.

At the age of 10 he was introduced to an experienced teacher who understood his challenges. Her caring but no-nonsense approach resulted in many battles inside and outside the classroom. But over the course of six months, with this teacher standing her ground, he began to come around and they formed a strong bond. In the last term of grade four he was still not reading or writing but he started to get involved in the classroom and engage in learning activities. Within six months his reading was at grade four level and six months after that he had caught up to his peers. Inside eighteen months he had absorbed five years of learning. His teacher/mentor was truly amazing, nonetheless his behaviour at times remained unacceptable. He was locked into a fixed pattern of conduct.

BECOMING ADAPTABLE

What?

By grade six his academic results were no longer a concern and for the first time in his life his auditory loop was filled with self-praise and pride. Now he just needed to work on his behaviour within social groups and during team activities. At the age of twelve he was introduced to the Organizational Zoo and he immediately recognised the animals and their behaviours in the book. He recalled certain events where he had behaved like the Rattlesnake and the Hyena, but more importantly he was able to reflect on the times when he had behaved appropriately, like an Owl or Ant might have in the situation.

How? (did OrgZoo activities help)

At this time a strategy was put in place for him to adopt the collaborative behaviour of certain animals such as Ants or Bees before entering settings that caused him stress. This guided him to make structured decisions about how he should behave. His application of the zoo characters was framing the impending situations in a positive light, which opened the door for alternative social conclusions.

Next an unexpected outcome presented itself, which became the catalyst for this piece. Not only did his behaviour improve dramatically, he actually began to mentor other children. He openly talked about the zoo animals and their behaviour. The intuitive nature and common language of the Organizational Zoo concepts meant that the other children could quickly understand. It was as if a light had suddenly been switched on. He now recognised that he could not change the behaviour of other people, only his own.

Outputs (tangible short-term value delivered)

A stable and productive life for the boy and his family and friends.

Outcome (intangible long-term value delivered)

One day after school he came home and said to his father, "I don't have a problem with my behaviour any more". And he was right. The power of the zoo metaphor was the final piece of the puzzle for positive change. The young man was growing up and starting to take responsibility for his actions.

Today he is in high school, making friends and doing well academically. He has a passion for singing, reading, maths and mythology. His imagination is wild and creative; the world is his oyster. There is no doubt that the Organizational Zoo helped this young boy navigate his way out of previously negative social situations. Understanding your behaviour and how it impacts others is the first step, understanding how to modify your own behaviour to get the best out of any situation is the key to success.

BECOMING ADAPTABLE

14. Lifestyle learning and value generation for others

This chapter is a final summary to remind you of some important aspects for your ongoing journey towards *Becoming Adaptable*.

Whilst acknowledging that nothing worthwhile in life is simple, these six summary reminders are useful for self-monitoring as your journey continues to emerge. Alone the reminders are insufficient to achieve your aims. However, they make a good set of subjective reflections to assess your progress over time. There is no end to this endeavour. We can always become better by being even more adaptable, as we experience a wider variety of situations. As we become adaptable, we become something a little different and gain insights into where we can then become more.

Monitoring achievements across these six aspects of your learning pathway will remind you of the progress you have made. Create a self-mentoring journal to record what you have done in each area. A journal illustrates your progress, maintains motivation, and reminds you that we do not know what the next steps are until we approach them.

BECOMING ADAPTABLE

Lifestyle learning to achieve your optimal social contributions

There is a lot of literature about lifelong learning and you have probably heard the term before. However, I want to talk about something else: lifestyle learning is an evolution of lifelong learning that happens within our chosen lifestyle. (Shelley and Goodwin 2018)

Learning in the modern world is becoming more informal and fragmented. People are learning from three-minute videos whilst commuting on a train and then engaging in conversations on social media about their new knowledge. Mobile devices and social media are being used in some formal learning environments to enhance the relevance and applicability of learning. The big tech companies like Apple, Google and LinkedIn have established 'universities' that offer a range of micro-credentialled learning experiences, and virtual learning is becoming a preferred way to develop. People are fitting learning into their hectic lifestyle.

Whether you like this, or not, grows less relevant as it becomes normalised. Practical micro-credentials are now being proudly displayed on social media as credible qualifications for employment, and employers and recruiters have started to acknowledge these. Lifestyle learning is here to stay, and formal traditional learning institutions are struggling to adapt to this new demand.

Developing beyond yourself to lead others

Ambling along inside your comfort zone about your own capabilities is easy enough. If you truly want to challenge yourself and make a bigger social contribution, consider leading others.

Leading typically places you into an elevated level of responsibility that is less clear. Being an effective leader requires listening to a wider range of perspectives and addressing more conflicting

14. Lifestyle learning and value generation for others

perspectives. Doing this well strengthens your adaptability as you work through the broader range of interacting challenges.

Stepping up to a leadership role does not have to happen in a workplace. There are many ways engage in developing others that are equally as rewarding for all involved. There is a lot to be learnt about adaptability from life roles such as parenting, supporting a friend through a crisis or a relative through late life, and leading from behind through charitable work. The more of these roles we engage in, the more we understand about our own capabilities. Sometimes we can surprise ourselves, in either direction. We thought we could easily do something, but struggle when it comes to implementing it. Alternatively, we were afraid of committing to an action or a relationship, but once started it comes easier than we expected.

The reward from engaging in such activities is the mutual benefit. My own capabilities have been developed far more through my support of others than by formal activities specifically targeted at developing my own capabilities. This is especially so in the areas of 'soft' skills and relationships. There is no better learning environment than working on specific challenges with others.

Organizational Zoo Ambassadors Network (OZAN)

The OrgZoo Ambassadors Network has been described elsewhere in this book (for example, Chapter 9) and online (organizationalzoo.com). Social support is a key success factor for self-development and the development of others. Finding others who are on similar paths to ourselves can be extremely helpful. This is not because you can simply copy someone who has already achieved a similar milestone. It is because you can share stories about a range of ways to get there and the barriers and accelerators available.

There are some excellent examples of international support communities doing great work for members. Two of my favourites are entirely voluntary: KM4Dev (wiki.km4dev.org) and SIKM

BECOMING ADAPTABLE

Leaders (sikm.groups.io). These two knowledge-sharing communities have active virtual forums in which people are sharing ideas and answering each other's questions, simply because they like to help each other and make a social contribution. Even if you are not a knowledge professional, visiting to watch the behaviour and inclusive social ecosystem is worthwhile. Stan Garfield, the founder of SIKM Leaders, has written an insightful book on the facilitation of communities (Garfield 2020).

Leading and inspiring willing intelligent followers

Adaptability is a significant characteristic of the modern (and future) successful leader. Just as engaging in inclusive leadership practices is a key aspect of *Becoming Adaptable*, your own confidence and adaptability can inspire others to engage with a worthy community or initiative. Challenging yourself to lead others is personally rewarding, beyond the financial rewards that may eventuate.

The benefits flowing from a leader's actions are amplified when motivated by mutual benefit, as this leads to stronger relationships that sustain over time. Putting yourself in such situations often provides for accelerated adaptability. Embedding such experiences into normal daily activities develops an expanding comfort zone and enhanced performance, and that becomes lifestyle learning.

Facilitating a safe-fail environment to build sustained trust

Lifestyle learning occurs in increasingly varied environments. Gone are the times in which learning happened in classrooms. In lifestyle learning every moment of every day can be a learning opportunity.

With mindFLEX, it becomes a habit to observe everything around you as you pass through all types of environment, contemplating what they mean for a range of perspectives. The random flow of observations is efficiently sorted and relevant observations converted into more meaningful insights. The parallel processing of observations enables the experienced facilitator to quickly see where risks are emerging and to take mitigating actions before those risks develop into issues.

The safe-fail approach (Snowden and Boone 2007) is superior to fail-safe, as you want people to have the confidence to explore and test possibilities. This requires the facilitator to create the atmosphere in which participants are outside their comfort zone but are not unsafe. This enables sharing of novel and incomplete ideas, enabling new insights to emerge and coalesce into potential options.

Trust is a foundation of a safe-fail environment. Participants need to trust they are safe so that they can interact constructively in the uncertainty. The more this happens, the more trust is developed, enabling the interactions to become more challenging.

Being part of developing new learning experiences and approaches

Being part of the development of new learning experiences challenges you to think beyond your current capabilities and knowledge.

When posed a challenge, people will naturally offer solutions that exist within their current realm of knowledge and experiences. This may not be the best path forward. Completely novel challenges may adequately, but not optimally, be served by existing options. Best options benefit from completely new approaches to exploring and then addressing the challenges.

The use of frameworks like Cynefin (en.wikipedia.org/wiki/Cyncfin _framework) and Agile (en.wikipedia.org/wiki/Agile _leadership) allows generation of diverse options that are more likely to provide better solutions. Aligned principles have been built into the

BECOMING ADAPTABLE

activities in Chapters 6 and 7 to enable facilitators to design and lead more open and appropriate learning activities.

Becoming adaptable

A simple way to start and monitor your adaptability and capabilities is to create yourself a diary with these six questions, based on the items discussed above.

Ask yourself — What have I done this week that has contributed to my:

1. Lifestyle learning and social contributions?
2. Development beyond my current comfort zone through leading others?
3. Using a creative way to amplify learning through a social network (such as OZAN)?
4. Inspiring someone to become a willing, intelligent follower (not necessarily of you)?
5. Facilitating a safe-fail environment that increased the trust in a relationship?
6. Creating a new way to stimulate learning, for myself or someone else?

This is not about keeping score for your ego or bragging to others about how good you are. It is to remind you to feel good about what you have achieved for yourself and others. This motivates you on your journey of becoming and reminds you how far you have come along the way. Sometimes we forget to acknowledge successes, just assuming what was done was necessary. This humility is an important characteristic of being a contributing person. However, dwelling on failure, and not balancing it with the value created from successes, augers for lower self-esteem and reduces your commitment to ongoing lifestyle learning.

14. Lifestyle learning and value generation for others

Don't expect to achieve a significant milestone on each of the six criteria every week. Some weeks you may not be able to recall any achievements for any of the criteria. Sometimes detailed stuff just needs to be done. However, if you get a series of such weeks, you then have to ask yourself if you are too embedded in tactical, reactive tasks. The answer may be that it is necessary right now. Be honest with yourself to determine how long is too long to remain in such an environment. It is always good to be adaptable and look for ways to make the situation better, to find alternatives that have better balance.

So now you have everything you need to become adaptable. I and members of OZAN are interested to hear your stories of how this goes and how you have adapted the approaches for your own contexts. I have great confidence that if you undertake a path that utilises the advice and activities described here you will be happier, healthier and feel more confident in your life. If you undertake this journey with others, it is more likely to achieve greater success and faster.

This may be the end of this book, but it also represents the acceleration of your *Becoming Adaptable* project. Hopefully you will go back over the relevant parts of this book in your activities and conversations as you diarise and discuss your experiences with others.

Enjoy *Becoming Adaptable*!

BECOMING ADAPTABLE

SUCCESS STORY
The Singapore 50-year celebration project

Arthur Shelley
OZAN Founder, International

Context (where and when)

The Singapore Government commissioned many projects in 2015 to celebrate fifty years of independence. One of these projects was to collect pioneer stories to capture what Singapore was like at the time of independence and provide some services to these pioneers.

It was a tremendous success and during the project those involved realised that the network and community they had created was a valuable asset for Singapore. However, the funding was only for a one-year project.

Why?

The purpose was to engage the team in a series of conversations to determine how to secure this group of people, their relationships and knowledge as on ongoing funded asset; that is, transform them into an advisory services organisation so that social benefits could be delivered ongoing.

Who?

This project had 238 staff who collectively facilitated the activities of 16,000 volunteers to implement the social project for the Singapore Government.

An Organizational Zoo Ambassador was asked to design an interaction for all team members to be involved in cocreating a path forward for this to happen.

What?

Two workshops were designed in association with the project management team. One day was allocated to take the leadership team of twenty through the planned activities and assess their perspective of the Behavioural DNA of the whole organisation. This was done to build their confidence as facilitators of the activities for the rest of the team.

These leaders then cofacilitated a similar series of activities over two days for the whole team (each working within smaller groups), with the OrgZoo Ambassador as the master facilitator coordinating the overall activities across groups and adding some additional strategic conversations the leaders had not yet seen.

How? (did OrgZoo activities help)

Both the leadership team and each of the sub-teams performed a Behavioural DNA of the current culture as well as for what they thought the future culture needed to be for the team to evolve into an ongoing organisation.

They discussed the differences between the two and considered what types of activities and projects they could perform to enable this evolution. They also considered what projects ideas they could propose to the Singapore government that might attract ongoing funding.

Over the next few weeks, all of these outputs were captured and built into a strategic plan, which was presented to the government decision makers.

Outputs (tangible short-term value delivered)

Behavioural DNA of the team — current and future (plus difference analysis).

BECOMING ADAPTABLE

List of cocreated projects for future implementation, with stated social value.

Strategic plan for the change from a one-year project team to an ongoing funded organisation.

Outcomes (intangible long-term value delivered)

The strategic proposal was accepted by the government and the project team became a permanent organisation. It has continued to evolve and has successfully implemented many social projects since that time, each with both tangible benefits and intangible social value. The Organizational Zoo enabled people in the project to make a mindset shift from tactical to strategic and adapt their behaviours to align the culture to what was required to enable this to happen.

Appendix

Concepts useful to professional facilitators

BECOMING ADAPTABLE

This Appendix lists nearly seventy concepts that a professional facilitator will benefit from understanding. A deep understanding of these concepts, and experiences in applying them in context, provides a rich mental resource to draw from in emergent facilitation activities.

Of course, it is possible to facilitate without knowledge of these concepts and not all of them are applicable to every conversation. However, it is likely the outputs and outcomes of your work will be richer when you are able to introduce a range of these concepts at the right moment in an interaction.

Which concept to include at what moment is entirely emergent. It depends on the participants, their experiences, the level of diversity and trust between them, and your style as a facilitator. Your ability to read the room and choose in the moment often determines the direction of the knowledge flow and the quality of the outcomes. Reflecting on your performance afterwards helps to enhance the next performance.

This list is not the only concepts that are important — there are more! Each professional facilitator could look at this list and suggest other concepts they consider more important. This highlights just how complex facilitation is, and why practicing mindFLEX is important to success. Facilitators need to be inside the heads and hearts of each participant and sense how to act in the most productive way in every moment, knowing that each participant may have a different expectation of what that should be. Every facilitation is different and each one is a performance on which you are judged. Do not be afraid of that: see it as motivation to enable those in your care to become adaptable!

This list is a brief introduction based on my own knowledge and experiences. Before using a concept, facilitators are advised to search for a range of articles on the topic, then engage in some critical analysis and reflective practice about what they read and discuss with others.

Appendix: useful concepts

Action

The most memorable and valuable learning and adaptation capability comes from doing. That is, putting things into action. The value to be created for learning comes from putting the learning insights into action in ongoing activities. For more insights, search Action Learning

Adaptability

The confidence and capability of being able to change to a range of alternatives in situations to achieve better outcomes. Applies to behaviour, ideas, culture and other aspects of personal and professional pursuits. For deeper insights, read this book (again).

Attitude

How you feel and how this influences your thinking. Is heavily influenced by past experiences and subliminal biases. Can be influenced by new experiences, maintaining a mindFLEX and your attitude towards diversity and learning.

Awareness

Your level of understanding what you observe, feel and sense, and how you interpret that. Awareness is elevated through being consciously aware of what you are interacting with and being open to a variety of interpretations.

Behaviour

How you engage with the world. The set of choices (conscious or subconscious) on a range of aspects guiding how we conduct ourselves in relationships. Includes actions, voice, body language, reactions, level of interest and respect. Aligned behaviours are the basis of sustainable relationships and inclusive culture.

BECOMING ADAPTABLE

Capability development

Increasing your abilities of knowing, doing and being, enabling you to perform at a higher level, more consistently and across more situations. It is achieved through learning and reflection on experiences. For deeper insights, start with *KNOWledge SUCCESSion*.

Change

A constant and accelerating state of the world and how we interact with it. Change is often met with resistance. However, it can be a stimulant of opportunity and innovation if addressed with a mindFLEX approach. There is a huge body of literature on change and several useful approaches to constructively address it.

Coaching

An approach to accelerating development and refining of skills. In contrast to mentoring, which is support around optimising one's life and career path goals. Developmental relationships are often a combination of both coaching and mentoring to develop a well-rounded and confident person/professional.

Collaboration

The act of openly engaging with others to achieve mutually beneficial outcomes. Often works well because it leverages the diversity of knowledge, skills and behaviours of a collective, making the collective more powerful and capable than individuals involved. Amplifies value cocreation because of the synergies generated when people interact with each other through creative friction and willingness to openly contribute knowledge and ideas.

Appendix: useful concepts

Complexity

The state in which interactions happen where multiple influencing factors are interacting in unpredictable and unrepeatable ways. This is the state in which most human interactions occur. A good starting point to understand characteristics of complexity and how it differs from other states is the Wikipedia entry on complex systems (en.wikipedia.org/wiki/Complex_system).

Confidence

Positive feeling about the level of capability and trust in oneself, other people or an object/situation. Self-confidence is an outcome of *Becoming Adaptable* and is a key influencing factor in resilience and success.

Conversation

A primary way in which people engage with each other to share ideas and insights. Ideally conversations can be positive, but they can be a negative experience if done badly. Best conversations are face-to-face experiences with an open mind and constructive intent. However, in the modern world, conversations can be enabled by tools to be asynchronous and remote. Conversations can be used for many purposes and the ways to facilitate conversations varies by situation. See *Conversations That Matter* in Chapter 6.

Creativity and cocreation

Creativity is the way in which we generate new ideas and things. It is a divergent activity that is accelerated when facilitated between a group of people who proactively engage in lateral thinking to leverage a diversity of concepts. Cocreation happens when people allow ideas to emerge an evolve between a range of people in an emergent environment.

BECOMING ADAPTABLE

Creativity is one of the World Economic Forum's list (2020) of top ten future skills.

Critical thinking

A clear, rational, open-minded cognitive process informed by evidence. There is a deep body of literature on critical thinking and ways to develop this capability. It has been in the top three top future skills in the World Economic Forum's list for the past decade.

Culture

The collective norms, expectations, values and behaviour of a group of people. It is often more accurately characterised by a deep understanding of observed behaviours, than by what is overtly stated. Understanding of behaviour can be cocreated by facilitating a Behavioural DNA activity by the people in the culture.

Curiosity

An inquisitiveness, driven by the desire to learn, know and understand more deeply. Although it can be to just satisfy self-interest, curiosity is a powerful driver for creativity, innovation and continuous improvement. It is the source of insightful questions that trigger divergent *Conversations That Matter*.

Data analysis

Traditionally data is considered to be a pure observation to define something — an object measure, or fact. However, in the human world many observations are subjective and open to interpretation. Understanding the sources, type and quality of data is essential to good data analysis. Data analysis is a complex combination of science and art that involves being aware of the limitations and assumptions that apply to how and when the data was generated.

Appendix: useful concepts

Decision making

People make decision all the time, sometimes consciously, with great deliberation and evidence and sometimes without much conscious thought or evidence. The science of decision making has developed significantly as data generation, management and analysis have advanced through technology and new approaches. Decisions are how people determine how to interact with the world in everything we do. This makes it a significant strategic investment to do well. The ways in which participants make decisions can vary significantly and influence how to interact with a diverse group. Not making a decision, or deciding to do nothing, is also a decision!

Design thinking

Design thinking (DT) is an inclusive, iterative approach to development and innovation. It has become popular in industries in which rapid change or development leads to competitive advantage. There is plenty of literature and a good starting point is IDEO (www.ideou.com/pages/design-thinking), one of the leading DT innovation organisations.

Emergence

The process of becoming visible or into prominence after being concealed. A new idea, thing or entity that is different from the original inputs emerges from interactions. Although a very old concept, emergence itself has emerged into more common use in creative and innovation pursuits. A facilitator benefits from a stimulating and emergent environment, and a start-up incubator usually tries to create an emergent ecosystem. See Santa Fe Institute's website (www.santafe.edu/research/results/working-papers/on-emergence-and-explanation)

BECOMING ADAPTABLE

Emotional intelligence

The ability to understand and act on one's own emotions and the ability to understand and act appropriately in relation to others' emotional state: that is, how capable one is at reading the emotional aspects of the environment and engaging with others to optimise the outcomes. EQ is a measure of a person's maturity level in emotional intelligence and can be increased with targeted development. Start with Goleman (2009) and his personal website (www.danielgoleman.info).

Engagement

A word with many meanings. In this context it is the act of being actively involved, or an assessment of the level of commitment one has for the situation. A facilitator seeks to engage the people in their activities in ways that stimulate a high level of interest and participation to generate optimal outcomes. Stakeholders should not be managed, they should be appropriately engaged. Engagement is a matter of inviting willing participation rather than attempting to control participants.

Ethics

A branch of philosophy dealing with values relating to human conduct, with respect to morals of a group or culture. Assessment that judges the degree of right and wrong of actions and motives. Ethical awareness is critical in facilitation as acceptability of practices varies across different cultures. Making ethical judgements about what activities are acceptable, although in the awareness that diversity of practice is present. The humorous rule of thumb for ethical assessment is, if you cannot proudly tell your grandmother what you did, it is probably not ethical.

Appendix: useful concepts

Humour

Humour is a powerful tool that can impact significantly in a situation — sometimes well (if appropriate) and sometimes very badly. Philosopher Edward de Bono stated that humour is the most under-utilised management tool. It can highlight creative insights, de-stress or depoliticise a situation and stimulate a fun environment. However, humour is context and culturally sensitive. Poor choice of humour can destroy relationships and cause conflict.

Identity and belonging

People like to have a sense of belonging. They identify with a desired group, place or culture and are proud of the connection. Identity and belonging are a deep part of who we consider ourselves to be. It influences our values, behaviour, decisions, actions and who we choose to interact with. People often introduce themselves in ways that highlight these connections. For example, I am Australian and from the outback; I am part of a community that serves society, et cetera. As a deeply personal aspect of a person's inner self, this is an aspect to be respected and can provide insights to how they may be expected to behave.

Impact

The effects and value generated by the activities, during and after the event. Impacts can be tangible or intangible, as well as positive or negative. Impact varies with different people involved, depending on their own prior experiences, expectations and perspectives and how well the facilitator engages with them.

Influence

Influence comes in many forms and the word can be a verb

BECOMING ADAPTABLE

(they influenced the crowd), a noun (she is a significant influencer in the party) or an adjective (the influencing factor is good behaviour). Influence is both a powerful asset and a significant action. A facilitator needs to be aware of the level of influence they have on a group of participants and all the ways in which others' influences are impacting the relationships and interactions in the event (and beyond).

Innovation

The actions or process through which ideas and concepts are refined to generate new products, processes or services. There are many ways to manage innovation that can be found in the huge body of literature over several decades.

Insights

Deep understanding of the true nature of a person or object that enables one to engage with it in a more meaningful, informed way. Insights help us to understand the inner truth of the thing or situation. Insights can come from intuition or be accelerated through deep reflective conversations with a range of people.

Knowledge

An intangible human characteristic that is developed through a lifetime of experiences and learning, producing the ability to inform decision making and actions.

A person's total knowledge is unique to them. Although aspects and insights from this knowledge can be shared with others, when this happens it may manifest itself in a different way because of the experiences of the recipient/s.

This is why diversity of people is critical to creativity and leadership. Their different perceptions of fact and states of knowing

Appendix: useful concepts

trigger a range of cognitive and emotional comprehensions. Well-facilitated conversations about these differences drive the cocreation of new knowledge and insights for all involved.

Language

A complex and culturally sensitive way to transfer meaning between people using words and gestures, expressed through oral, movement and written forms. Although language is a powerful and essential part of communication, it is also highly symbolic. This means it is easily mis-expressed or misinterpreted. Although we think we are clear when we say or write something, that sense and meaning may not be correctly understood when another party receives and interprets the signal.

Leadership

The act of influencing others to become willing, considered followers of your cause (refer to my book, KNOWledge SUCCESSion). A genuine leader does not control people to implement their instructions; instead they positively engage people to act by being a role model. Followers are willing because they want to act in the way a leader recommends and have logically and emotionally aligned with these actions.

Learning

The acts, experiences and processes through which we become more capable across knowing, doing and being. *Becoming Adaptable* is a learning experience refined over time and honed through practice. Optimal learning is social, inclusive, collaborative and cocreative. It can be achieved through informal or formal interactions, face to face or virtual. Learning together with others amplified the learning experience and the quality of the outcomes.

BECOMING ADAPTABLE

Mentoring

A relationship through which a person of more experience guides the development of a less experienced person to enhance their capabilities and confidence to make decisions and act. This is not age related, as it is possible for a younger person to have more experience at something than an elder (such as technology competence). The relationship is more effective when there are mutual benefits and ongoing exploration of life outcomes, not just a focused on a set of skills (as in coaching).

Narrative

A mix of art, science and social connection, facilitated to create stories that share insights and inform a target audience. Narrative comes in a range of forms, such as an academic thesis or informal verbal stories. Humans relate to narratives and extract meaning from them in richer ways than other forms of communication. Story-telling seems to have emerged at roughly the same time as language: it has evolved as part of our human nature.

Opportunity creation

Opportunity creation is a positive way to engage with the world, an alternative to regarding challenges as problems to be fixed. If we see the benefits of changing something to improve the possibilities, we approach the challenge with a divergent mindset. This mindset enables many more possibilities to be cocreated, rather than finding an existing answer that may not be effective. See *KNOWledge SUCCESSion* for more detail on this type of mindFLEX.

Appendix: useful concepts

Optimism

The disposition to see the more favourable possibilities in situations and the ability to act constructively from a positive frame of mind, even if there are challenges.

Outcomes

Outcomes are the intangible, and typically longer-term, results of something: an event, conversation, project, relationship, et cetera. Outcomes are different from tangible outputs. Refer to *Conversations That Matter* (Chapter 6).

Outputs

Outputs are the tangible, and typically shorter-term, results of something like an event, conversation, project, or relationship. This is in contrast to the intangible outcomes. Refer to *Conversations That Matter* (Chapter 6).

Ownership

Ownership in this context is far more than legal possession of an object. It is taking responsibility and care to invest in an initiative or relationship in a deep and meaningful way: to feel fully accountable for the activities, and for the outputs and outcomes they generate, and to provide all the resources required to ensure they are successful.

People

We all know what people are and that they are critical! People are the central elements in relationships, creating new insights and implementing them. It is people who engage in behaviour, and some even become adaptable. The way people interact and the ecosystems in which this happens are essential to sustained high performance. However, people need to be specifically mentioned as, despite their

BECOMING ADAPTABLE

importance, they are often not engaged with appropriately. Something is wrong when people are used as a resource or, worse, overlooked, rather than respected as the body and soul of high performance.

Performance

Performance has two critical aspects. First, every facilitation is a performance. It is a form of live entertainment, engagement and learning. As with every performance, judgements are inevitable, even if only in the minds of participants. Facilitators gather feedback so that they can see how to improve their performance next time.

Second, performance itself is a measure of the quality of work. Facilitation is most often done to improve the performance of a person, a team or an organisation. Performance measures are applied and most organisations use key performance indicators (KPIs) to actively monitor performance over time. (Granted, many do this badly and KPIs are gamed, but that is another conversation).

Everything we do comes back to performance, even in intangible factors like relationships. As facilitators, we need to consider our own performance and how we enhance the performance of those we serve. *Becoming Adaptable* is a way of enhancing both.

Perspectives

Perspective is the view a person comes to about what they are observing, and it is the way they came to this view. All perspectives are in some way biased. Once we understand that there are many possible perspectives on any situation, we are able to leverage this diversity of views. Believing that there is only one way to interpret something is an invitation to failure. The more absolute and rigid we become, the less

Appendix: useful concepts

resilient we are. Practising mindFLEX is a good way to move forward and become adaptable. There is a lot of discussion about perspectives in this book as well as a good body of literature available.

Pitch

Another one of these words (see *language*, above) with many meanings, mostly not relevant here. In this context, pitch refers to throwing an idea or proposal into a conversation in order to generate discussion or secure agreement. A facilitated activity might conclude with a pitch for capital investment in a start-up business, or a pitch for approval and resources to proceed with a project idea. Successful pitching is a key skill for a facilitator because the ideas developed in an interaction go nowhere unless there is some sort of pitch at the end to get them applied. A facilitator needs to pitch their own business well to survive commercially; while working with a group, a pitch for the facilitator's planned activities aims to secure engagement. See my book *KNOWledge SUCCESSion* for advice on structuring an engaging pitch.

Problem solving

Often seen as a frustrating aspect of professional life, problem solving is a strong motivator for many people. It is a challenge for the mind and attracts kudos when successfully implemented. This double endorphin hit stimulates managers to work hard. Those who can resolve problems quickly and efficiently are seen as positive contributors and are promoted to higher positions. Traditionally the practices of problem solving were focused on critical analysis skills and tools, but more recently the benefits of creative divergent approaches have demonstrated their value.

BECOMING ADAPTABLE

Process

Clear, stepped-out ways of doing something. Processes are excellent for making sure that the best practices — a well proven path known to generate the expected output — are done correctly. There are parts of the modern world that appropriately remain in the domain of well designed, implemented and monitored processes. These include areas like risk management, occupational health and safety, space exploration, nuclear facility management. In other words, areas in which the consequences of not doing things properly are potentially harmful or fatal.

Professionalism

Operating to a high standard of ethics, capabilities and behaviour. Professionalism is a key influencing factor for reputation and an important influence on the relationships one can attract and build.

Project management

Projects have become the main vehicle of change and capability development for individuals, teams and organisations. Three decades ago, the emphasis was on process to keep things operating smoothly and in the right way. Now the world changes so quickly, professionals shift from one project to another to design, develop and implement new products, services and ways to get things done. Projects are now done in many organisations with Agile (more flexible and iterative) approaches, which involve more facilitation of interactions than traditional project management. For more detail on the importance of projects and how they are facilitated, refer to my book *KNOWledge SUCCESSion*.

Appendix: useful concepts

Quality

The best definition of quality is 'fit for purpose,' although this is not how it is used in general conversation. Quality is often associated with a dichotomy of high or low, or cheap verses luxury. It needs a more sophisticated assessment. A high quality solution is one that matches the requirements perfectly. High quality facilitation is achieved when the interactions align with the level of competency and expectations of the participants. There is no sense in using highly academic language and concepts when facilitating a tactical, pragmatic team who are working on a practical solution. An ill-informed trainer may feel that fancy language makes them seem clever, but the reality is they fail to engage the participants in a way that accelerates successful outcomes. A high quality facilitator understands the expectations and adjusts what they do, and how, according to the desired outcomes.

Reflective practice

Investing the time to deeply consider the implications of potential outcomes and how to act to achieve the best possible results. Traditionally reflection focused on past action (looking back at past actions) or in current action (as you are acting). Increasingly it is important to reflect forward, to consider a range of possible actions to take in the future. Reflective practice is a critical element of all facilitation, especially through conversations before, during and after activities. Significant learning happens for participants in the reflective conversations after an activity. If these are rushed, the facilitator reduces the value being cocreated in their event. Games (or any capability development activity) without reflective practice may be fun, but they are limited in the value they create.

BECOMING ADAPTABLE

Relationships

Humans build their identity and sense of belonging through the relationships they have. This is true of personal and professional life. Relationships are the core knowledge asset in your value network. You are as powerful or as weak as the level of trust in these relationships.

Relationships are not measured by how many friends or contacts you are connected to in social and professional applications. Links between people (and teams and organisations) are far deeper and more important than that. The nature, level of trust, and degree of interdependency in the connection indicate its real strength and value. Often your reputation is heavily influenced by the visible, strong connections you have in your network. This can be either a positive or a negative impact.

Reputation

The collective outcome of the judgements people make about you or the entity in question. This is based on your trustworthiness, ethical conduct, capabilities, style, effectiveness, professionalism and almost every other factor in this list (directly or indirectly).

Reputation is your key commercial and personal asset. It is built slowly through demonstrated practice and relationships with others. It can be immediately destroyed by one poor act that undermines your credibility or integrity. A facilitator who consistently acts in ways to generate a positive and trusted reputation attracts more work and delivers higher quality.

Appendix: useful concepts

Risks

A risk is something that might happen that has a detrimental impact. This is different from an issue, which is something that IS happening. The two key aspects of risk are probability and consequence. Probability is the chance that the risk occurs. Consequence is the impact if that risk does become an issue.

Risk mitigation is an important aspect of facilitation. In current professional practice and our increasingly litigious society, many clients expect risk insurance to be taken before contracts can be signed. This shows the negative impact of two factors: increasing uncertainty and lowered trust. There is a large body of literature on risk and many management approaches are available.

Role models

A role model is a person or entity who consistently demonstrates the actions and behaviours you respect and desire to emulate. Being a positive role model with a strong reputation is critical for a facilitator. Participants in a program are more likely to follow and engage with someone they can identify with and respect.

In our hyperconnected, international society, armed with video recording and sharing mobile devices, the consistency of a person's professional behaviour is important. Being a respected role model is challenging if dubious aspects of your life or professional practice are splashed over social media. Everyone can be a role model to someone — some you desire to follow and others you definitely do not wish to. Political role models are a good example of this: someone viewed as a positive role model on one side of politics may be considered negatively by the other side.

BECOMING ADAPTABLE

Security

Security is not an obvious candidate for this list of important factors for facilitators. It can relate to physical security for you in regions where violence can result from shared perspective that differ from the authorities. An extreme example is a leader of the opposition in an authoritarian society being incarcerated for facilitating conversations that criticise the government. Facilitators invited to engage with international events can face this challenge, especially if they are advocating leading-edge ideas and approaches.

Data and information security are also worth your attention. A facilitator may be sharing protected intellectual property and engaging participants in unique approaches in their events. The content and insights from this are easily and instantly shared through social media platforms in ways that make content security almost impossible. Protecting yourself, your ideas and approaches is a significant challenge for some facilitators. The intellectual property (IP) represents your value and influences your reputation. Whilst you can ask that people respect your IP, security breaches are common and costly to reverse. This may reduce the financial rewards you receive for your investment in capabilities. More importantly, if your IP and brand are used badly by others your reputation can be significantly damaged. This could be caused by deliberate malice, plain theft, or complete ignorance on behalf of the other party.

Sensemaking

The process by which one extracts meaning from observations and experiences. It describes how an individual or group can develop a deeper understanding of a situation or thing through observation, reflection and analysis. The sensemaking process is ongoing and ventures beyond measurable facts to

Appendix: useful concepts

include aspects such as emotional, social and behavioural characteristics of what happened or is happening.

Sensemaking is more interested in stimulating the emergence of plausibility and influencing factors than about determining a singular truth.

The Wikipedia entry on sensemaking (en.wikipedia.org/wiki/Sensemaking) is a good place to start making sense of sensemaking.

Social cocreation

Generating a range of hybrid options from social interactions. One cannot cocreate alone; it requires others to engage with you. This socialisation of ideas between people as they engage in collaborative sensemaking generates richer and more diverse outputs and outcomes. This is discussed extensively throughout this book.

Stakeholders

People or entities that are affected positively or negatively by the initiative you are facilitating. Stakeholder engagement (often called stakeholder management — misguidedly, because you are better to influence than to control them) is a fine blend of leadership, planning, communication and collaboration. Almost inevitably in significant initiatives, stakeholders will be represented across a spectrum from strong supporters through to strong advocates against your initiative. How to deal with this diversity of stakeholders is covered in my book *KNOWledge SUCCESSion* and a range of high quality professional literature.

Storytelling

Sharing of stories in a way the engages people with the meaning and principles of what you are sharing. Stories have

BECOMING ADAPTABLE

been part of all human cultures since ancient times. Fairy tales are a good example of how cultural principles have been shared for eons. Storytelling is a highly influential way to share insight and influence people. Stories are more credible if they are real and personalised. Constructed, plausible stories are also used to influence people.

Succession

At the most basic level this is a sequence of activity that results in transfer of thoughts, responsibilities, capabilities, knowledge and authorities over time from one person or entity to another. It can relate to people, roles and other aspects of professional and personal pursuit. In this specific context, succession is crucial as a way of building capabilities and retaining knowledge to minimise losses and optimise performance. This is especially important as the workforce becomes more mobile: critical insights, experiences and know-how can be permanently lost if strategic succession plans are not proactively invested in. My book *KNOWledge SUCCESSion* is the best place to start to explore this topic.

Sustainability

The ability to ensure ongoing outcomes can be achieved in the long-term without causing detrimental impacts. This requires solid critical analysis of the whole lifecycle impact of the product, activity or practices in question, taking a system thinking perspective. This is important in many aspects of professional life and our wider systems such as environmental harmony. Sustainability of businesses is also a key factor in strategic planning. A facilitator benefits from being aware of balancing short-term and long-term impacts to ensure the practices emerging are sustainable. A common challenge is that an extraction mindset (immediate benefit focus) overrides

Appendix: useful concepts

a contribution mindset (adopting sufficient protections or investing back into the system as a whole to ensure sustainability).

Trust

Confidence in the honesty, credibility and integrity of a person, relationship or thing. Trust is a very personal characteristic that exists between a trustor (the person, group or entity investing trust in another) and the trustee, to meet their agreed expectations. Trust is the foundation of relationships and a social requirement to engage with any party on a significant endeavour. Trust helps to mitigate against risk because we feel more confident dealing with people we believe to be reliable and who will interact with us with integrity.

Trust can be deferred to others, which is what happens when we ask someone we trust to recommend someone they trust. This is why reputation and word of mouth is critical to social networks. Building trust in a community or team provides a strong sense of connection and harmony. However, when trust is broken it is extremely difficult to repair the relationship.

Trust is an important asset for all people in personal and professional relationships and is the currency of knowledge flow in organisations. We will openly share with people we trust, but are reluctant to share or interact with people we don't trust. Some people make the mistake of giving trust easily and get damaged by the poor outcomes. Many untrustworthy scams target these trusting people as they are easier targets to extract value from.

A facilitator benefits from developing trust by sharing a few things about themselves and encouraging participants to

BECOMING ADAPTABLE

share with each other. This sharing behaviour accelerates the building of trust.

Trusted advisor

The ultimate status of a relationship between an advisor and their client, as described by David Maister (2002; 2021). Once the relationship reaches this peak level there is significant mutual benefit for the advisor and the client, because the of level of trust and respect between each other. A facilitator can develop a strong relationship with clients and create the foundations of trusted advisor status with a group they collaborate with over time. Such relationships can stimulate high performance sustained over a long period of time.

Value

A measure of relative worth, merit, or importance that can take many forms. The most common token of tangible value exchange is money, but values can be expressed in terms of the amount of other things for which it can be exchanged. Intangible value is critical in social relationships, such as moral support for someone in need, sincere advice shared with integrity, or simply a thank you acknowledging a job well done. People are more likely to appreciate and be positively influenced by an authentic acknowledgement of the value they add than by some token tangible payment.

Value exchange is important to motivation and engagement. The concept of reciprocity is a key influence in most cultures. Relationships are kept alive when there is a perception of fair value exchange by all parties in the relationship.

Relationships in which any party feels the exchange of value is not fair are unlikely to be sustainable.

Appendix: useful concepts

Value is a deep component of philosophies, mindsets and cultures. A capitalist has a value extraction mindset: their focus is how much value they can extract from an opportunity for them or their stakeholders. A social philanthropist has a value contribution mindset more focused on the value they can add or create for others.

Visualisation

Two forms of visualisation are important in facilitation. One is the graphic expression of data or concepts to highlight the messages they represent. Big data has accelerated the development of tools for creating images that convey meaning for the body of data available. This visualisation enables more people to understand the evidence behind the data, that they cannot easily discover from the pure data.

The second form of visualisation is the ability to visualise possible solutions that do not yet exist. Good facilitation about emergent possibilities in a cocreative ecosystem enables the social interaction of ideas and sensemaking to generate new possibilities in the minds of the participants. That is, the conversations and interactions enable a person to visualise a future product, service or state and this visualisation activity generates new options and opportunities. The early stages of this experience rely heavily on imagination-fuelled conversation. The expression of the ideas that emerge from such interactions can be in graphic or other forms.

The field of visualisation (in both forms) has developed rapidly in the past decade and benefits from new technologies and computer graphic capabilities.

BECOMING ADAPTABLE

Volatile, uncertain, complex and ambiguous (VUCA)

VUCA is a term that came from military training to describe the environment of the battlefield and ways to act in it. It has entered general professional practice over the past decade because of the increased unpredictability and short action/reaction cycles that now apply in business and government. The accelerating rate of change, driven by technology and customer expectations, has made VUCA increasingly relevant to professional and personal decision making.

Acknowledgements

Anyone can write a book; it is not that hard to fill pages with words. However, it takes a community engaged in conversations over time, to cocreate a magic book. This book was contemplated and written in pieces over many years and conversations with a diversity of people. The final product in front of you is more useful than it would have been if it were quickly written from a single perspective and with little input or feedback from others.

This book is an outcome of applying many of the concepts and ideas that it shares. It is the product of conversations between members of the OrgZoo international community, our clients' and other interested parties. It emerged as we curiously experimented, collaborated, cocreated and reflected. Ideas became options, which were developed into repeatable techniques that created value for our workshop participants.

I am deeply thankful to all the people who have shared their perspectives about conscious choice of behaviour and how to achieve this in practice. *Knowing, Doing, Being* and *Becoming*

BECOMING ADAPTABLE

Adaptable is transformational for both personal and professional aspects in life. *Becoming Adaptable* happens because we have applied the ideas in constructive interactions with each other and engaged in reflective conversations about the impacts we observe.

The people who contributed to this book are too numerous to be individually listed here. Some have actively contributed like the OrgZoo practitioners and ambassadors who have shared stories of using these ideas in their practices, and clients who have shared endorsements for this book. Others have unknowingly contributed by making a remark or asking a remarkable question in a workshop that triggered the development of a new idea, technique or approach. These insights have generated adapted ways for design and facilitation of existing concepts and sometimes stimulated new ones.

These are some people who deserve specific mention and thanks. The OrgZoo Ambassadors have been terrific support from the beginning and remain active mentors for the OrgZoo international community. These are: Andrew (AJ) Dulaney Shaw, Keith De La Rue, Laurel Sutton, Frank Connolly, Mark Boyes, Tom Blair, Peter Renner, Nicole Stoecker, Vadim Shiraev, MD Indera Tasprin and Netpreeya Musigchai.

Mark Boyes has invested significant time taking up the role formerly filled by original artist John Szabo. He has added new images to support the ongoing development of the concept, including those in this book. He converted the original Organizational Zoo book to create the ebook version, and initiated the Educational Zoo project to provide a children's version of the concept activities. Keith De La Rue and Laurel Sutton have been actively involved in maintaining the online OrgZoo resources knowledge base to house files and documentation for the community. AJ Dulaney Shaw developed the macros to autogenerate the Behavioural DNA images, saving us enormous time and enabling this to be turned around within a workshop for deeper conversations. Tom Blair has been a strong supporter of applying OrgZoo into vocational

Acknowledgements

education programs, including the development of an award-winning program for construction site managers. Peter Renner and Nicole Stoecker translated the original book into German, designed the German language version of the OrgZoo character cards and maintain the OrgZoo Europe website. Vadim Shiraev facilitated the Russian translation of the OrgZoo character cards and included the activities into international events led from Russia. MD Indera Tasprin was active in designing and facilitating creative adaptations for the Singapore and Indonesian market, to extend the reach of the programs, as Netpreeya Musigchai did in Thailand. Frank Connolly and Laurel Sutton were instrumental in supporting the ideas in the early development days by providing opportunities to facilitate workshops using the concepts, enabling the ideas to evolve through application and feedback.

It truly takes a global village to raise a concept and support its development into maturity. Practitioners in the OrgZoo community have also played an active part of this development by using the techniques and sharing their feedback and ideas. A huge thank you to all these people, who I hope continue to use the approaches and further develop them.

This book started as a title over a decade ago, but it was never completely clear just what to include and what to leave out. There was so much to share, the first draft was a tome of interesting ideas, concepts, images and opportunities. I am deeply indebted to my editor, Margaret Ruwoldt for her editing and typesetting skills, especially her ability to see the relevant pieces among the large volume of 'stuff.' Margaret invested the time to talk through the meaning and purpose of what I was wishing to share and provided insights into how to put the pieces of the jigsaw together. This has ensured the book flows and informs in an enjoyable way, as a professional book should. Working through someone else's thinking, to sort what is most relevant to others, is quite a challenge, especially considering how my mind tends to jump between seemingly disconnected points at times. The readers, leaders,

BECOMING ADAPTABLE

mentors, coaches and practitioners who are using ideas and activities from this book can do so more easily and effectively because of Margaret's refining. Thank you from me, and in advance on behalf of our readers.

Finally, thank you to my family and friends. My twenty-year obsession with the development of these concepts has meant many hours sitting in a room, alone or in conversation with collaborators, thinking through the next stage of development and how the concepts can be adapted to help others develop their capabilities. Joy, my life partner, has patiently waited for me to return to Earth and get home tasks done on many occasions without complaint. My daughters Cath and Helen have always enthusiastically supported my creative, and perhaps sometimes eccentric, thoughts and activities. You are the source of my inspiration and purpose. Without your support, none of this would have been created.

Dr Arthur W Shelley

Melbourne, September 2021

References

Articles on the Organizational Zoo website:
— aligning behaviours
 organizationalzoo.com/aligning-behaviour-for-optimal-sharing
— building trusted relationships around common concerns
 organizationalzoo.com/reflecting-on-behaviour-for-team-success
— leveraging differences
 organizationalzoo.com/understanding-and-mitigating-culture-clash
— fuelling creativity and driving innovation
 organizationalzoo.com/behavioural-dna-of-creativity-part-2

Kevin Allen and Michael JD Sutton (2019) Emotify! The power of the human element in game-based learning, serious games and experiential education. Independently published. ISBN 978-1704604688

BECOMING ADAPTABLE

Chinmay Ananda (2016) FUNdamentals of financial statements: it's easier than you think. Independently published. ISBN 978-1728681320

Anonymous (2016, 2020) The evolution of a misquotation. Article at Darwin Correspondence Project. University of Cambridge: UK. Article published 25 November 2016, updated 23 April 2020. Available at www.darwinproject.ac.uk/people/about-darwin/six-things-darwin-never-said/evolution-misquotation

Alex Bennet, David Bennet, Arthur Shelley, Theresa Bullard, John Lewis (2019). The intelligent social change journey [Foundation for the Possibilities that are YOU! series]. Mountain Quest Institute: MQI Press: West Virginia. ISBN 9781949829235

Svend Brinkmann, Michael Hviid Jacobsen, and S⁻ren Kristiansen (2014) Historical overview of qualitative research in the social sciences. In Patricia Leavy (ed.) The Oxford handbook of qualitative research (1st edn). Oxford University Press. DOI: 10.1093/oxfordhb/9780199811755.013.017

David Chan (ed.) (2014) Individual adaptability to changes at work: new directions in research. Taylor & Francis Ltd: Routledge: London. ISBN 9780415832915

Oli Conner (2015, 2018) The history of qualitative research. Blog post available at oliconner.medium.com/the-history-of-qualitative-research-f6e07c58e439

References

Richard Crisp (2015). The social brain: how diversity made the modern mind. London: Robinson (Little, Brown Book Group). ISBN 9781472120236

Ann V Deaton (2018). VUCA tools for a VUCA world: developing leaders and teams for sustainable results. Glen Allen, Virginia: DaVinci Resources LLC. ISBN 9780692074947

Carol Dweck (2008) Mindset: the new psychology of success. Ballantine Books. ISBN 978-0345472328

Michael Fuchs, Jochen Messner, Rob Sok (2019) Leadership in a VUCA world. Zeitgeist Coaching and Training. ISBN 9780648500902

Stan Garfield (2020) Handbook of community management: a guide to leading communities of practice. De Gruyter Saur: Berlin. ISBN 9783110673555

Daniel Goleman (2009) Emotional intelligence: why it can matter more than IQ. Random House USA: Bantam Books: New York. ISBN 9780553383713

History.com editors (2010, 2021) Gandhi's first act of civil disobedience. Article at www.history.com/this-day-in-history/gandhis-first-act-of-civil-disobedience first published 21 July 2010, updated 4 June 2021. A&E Television Networks LLC: New York.

David H Maister, Robert Galford, Charles Green (2021) The trusted advisor: 20th anniversary edition. Free Press. ISBN 9781982157104

BECOMING ADAPTABLE

Max McKeown (2012) Adaptability: the art of winning in an age of uncertainty. Kogan Page Ltd: London. ISBN 9780749465247

Curtis Ogden (24 October 2017) Thinking like a Network 2.0. Blog post at Interaction Institute for Social Change. Available at interactioninstitute.org/thinking-like-a-network-2-0

Jeffrey Pfeffer and Robert Sutton (1999) The knowing-doing gap: how smart companies turn knowledge into action. Harvard Business Review Press: Boston. ISBN 9781578511242

Christof Rapp (2010) Aristotle's rhetoric. The Stanford Encyclopedia of Philosophy, spring 2010 edition, Edward N Zalta (ed). Available at plato.stanford.edu/entries/aristotle-rhetoric

Ken Robinson and Lou Aronica (2016) Creative schools: revolutionizing education from the ground up. Penguin Press. ISBN 9780141978574

Donald A Schön (1983) The reflective practitioner. Basic Books: London. ISBN 9780465068784

Arthur W Shelley (2007) The organizational zoo: a survival guide to workplace behaviour. Aslan Publishing: Santa Rosa, USA. ISBN 9780944031469. Second edition published 2021 by Intelligent Answers: Melbourne, ISBN 9780648461616 (ebook), 9780648461623 (print)

Arthur W Shelley (2009) Being a successful knowledge leader: what knowledge practitioners need to know to make a

References

difference. Globe Law and Business: Ark Group.
ISBN 9781906355456

Arthur W Shelley (2012) Metaphor as a means to constructively influence behavioural interactions in project teams. Doctor of Philosophy (PhD) thesis, RMIT University, Melbourne. Available at researchrepository.rmit.edu.au/esploro/outputs/9921861601701341

Arthur W Shelley (2017) KNOWledge SUCCESSion: sustained performance and capability growth through strategic knowledge projects. Business Expert Press: New York. ISBN 9781631571589

Arthur W Shelley (2018) Leading knowledge flows and cocreation for sustained future outcomes. Chapter 10 (page 189) in John Girard and JoAnn Girard (eds) Knowledge management matters: words of wisdom from leading practitioners. Independently published. ISBN 978-1974403196

Arthur W Shelley (2020a) Cocreated projects worth doing: an inclusive collaborative approach for design of strategic initiatives in VUCA. Journal of Technology & Governance, 1(1). Available at creactos.org/index.php/jtg/article/view/9

Arthur W Shelley (2020b). Reverse Bloom: A new hybrid approach to experiential learning for a new world. Journal of Education, Innovation and Communication (JEICOM) vol.2, issue 2, December 2020. PDF available at coming.gr/wp-content/uploads/2020/12/2_December2020_JEICOM_FINAL_Arthur-W-Shelley.pdf.

Arthur W Shelley and David Goodwin (2018). Optimising learning outcomes through social co-creation of new knowledge in real-life client challenges. Journal of Applied Learning and Teaching (JALT) vol.1 no.2. doi.org/10.37074/jalt.2018.1.2.4

Simon Sinek (2011) Start with why: how great leaders inspire everyone to take action. Penguin Books Ltd: London. ISBN 9780241958223

David J Snowden and Mary E Boone (2007) A leader's framework for decision making. Harvard Business Review, November. Available at hbr.org/2007/11/a-leaders-framework-for-decision-making

Jia Tolentino (23 March 2016) On the origin of certain quotable 'African proverbs'. Article at jezebel.com/on-the-origin-of-certain-quotable-african-proverbs-1766664089

World Economic Forum (August 2020) Human capital as an asset: an accounting framework to reset the value of talent in the new world of work. Available at www.weforum.org/reports/human-capital-as-an-asset-an-accounting-framework-to-reset-the-value-of-talent-in-the-new-world-of-work

About the author

Dr Arthur Shelley is collaborative community builder and learning facilitator and creative education designer with over 30 years of professional experience across the international corporate, government and tertiary education sectors.

He is an international author, has worked in 12 countries, is a mentor in several international communities, and has supervised PhD candidates in five countries. He has collaborated with

organisations as diverse as NASA, Cirque Du Soleil, local and national governments, universities, start-ups, SMEs and multinational corporations.

Arthur is acknowledged internationally as a knowledge and capability development thought leader, project manager and community builder. He has written three books prior to *Becoming Adaptable*, as well as chapters of collaborative book projects and a range of peer reviewed research papers, and is a reviewer for academic journals.

Arthur is the producer of international events such as Creative Melbourne and AuSKM. He is a regular international conference speaker, multi-award-winning tertiary teacher, and a mentor/career advisor for students and PhD candidates. He is the lead assessor of the Knowledge Ready Organisation Awards, a program initiated by the Knowledge Management Society of Singapore to take organisations on a journey of sustained performance improvement, based on knowledge informed strategic projects.

Arthur created and facilitated the Executive MBA capstone course for the Graduate School of Business and Law at RMIT University in Melbourne. This applied learning experience is based on

BECOMING ADAPTABLE

developing options for genuine client projects in industry and government to improve their productivity.

Arthur engages in collaborative research through his role as a Senior Industry Fellow at RMIT and was the former Global Knowledge Director of Cadbury Schweppes.

About the illustrator

Dr Mark Boyes EMBA is the Head of Healthcare Innovation at Australian Pharmaceuticals Industries based in Melbourne, Australia.

Mark holds an Executive MBA (Distinction) and a PhD in innovation and creativity. He has over 15 years of leadership experience in leading diverse teams in healthcare, information technology and business transformation. During his research Mark was a lecturer in technology and innovation strategy and design thinking at RMIT's Graduate School of Business and Law.

Mark's experience is broad, having worked across numerous sectors including security, finance, retail, gaming, fast-moving consumer goods, pharmaceuticals, and human resources. Mark has co-developed world's first technologies in the surveillance arena and more recently has been leading multi-million-dollar business intelligence and healthcare start-up projects. Mark has facilitated innovation and visualisation sessions in organisations such as NASA, RMIT University, Bangkok University, Hemisphere Design School in France, Creative Melbourne and Creative Bangkok.

Mark is a published author and illustrator with contributions to the Palgrave *Handbook of Workplace Innovation*, *The Organizational Zoo*, *KNOWledge SUCCESSion* and *Becoming Adaptable*.

BECOMING ADAPTABLE

The Organizational Zoo
A survival guide to workplace behaviour

2nd edition with new foreword

by Dr Arthur Shelley

Illustrated by John Szabo

Republished in 2021 to celebrate the release of *Becoming Adaptable*

Available in paperback and epub formats from your favourite bookshops worldwide and via www.organizationalzoo.com

www.ingramcontent.com/pod-product-compliance
Lightning Source LLC
Chambersburg PA
CBHW050305010526
44107CB00055B/2111